PERSPECTIVE
PERCEPTION
PERSEVERANCE

John Patterson

SPORTS
PUBLISHING
GROUP★★★★★

Perspective, Perception, Perseverance

©2020 by John Patterson

Published by Clovercroft Publishing, Franklin, Tennessee

Edited by OnFire Books

Copy Edit by David Brown

Cover Design by Nelly Sanchez

Interior Design by Suzanne Lawing

Printed in the United States of America

978-1-7340850-0-6

To Shannon, for giving me hope.

To Palmer, for giving me purpose.

CONTENTS

INTRODUCTION

Do you know who you want to be? I knew exactly *what* I wanted to do, but I never considered *who* I wanted to be. Most people spend their whole lives trying to find their purpose and their passion. I knew at just nine years old what I wanted to do. My dad came home from work one day, and I looked at my dad and told him, "I am going to play professional baseball when I grow up." With the help of my family, I became the fifth overall pick in the first round to the Montreal Expos in the 1996 Major League Baseball Draft and the first high school player drafted that year. I succeeded at my goal of *what* I wanted to do but lost *who* I was as a human being in the process. Baseball became my identity and with it came addiction, depression, and sadness. This is a story of success, failure, and my journey to learn who I am and my purpose in life.

In life, certain traits are non-negotiable to be a well-balanced, happy, and successful person. If you have the right perspective, the correct perception of yourself, and the ability to persevere, you can get through any situation life throws your way. Focusing on the positives in your life and being grateful give you the right perspective. Acknowledging that you are human and are not perfect will give you the correct perception and the ability to forgive yourself. Finally, having perseverance will allow you to never give up and to fight through life's ups and downs.

In building the life I wanted for myself, I lost balance. Too much of any one thing is not a good thing. Working too much. Drinking too much. Eating too much. Losing focus on what's truly important in life is so easy to do today. We are overloaded every single day with what success is supposed to look like. We are told we are failing if we are not meeting certain milestones at specific times. We have the ability to compare our lives to the lives of our "friends" in real time on social media, and we wonder why we become distracted or depressed. We put so much pressure on ourselves that we lose our ability to enjoy life. All these issues need to be addressed in our lives to gain a correct view of what success means to you. Success is defined differently for everyone and reached at different times for each individual. We should not make comparisons to other people's lives.

There is something we all have in common, and that is that we all want to figure "it" out. We want to feel as though we know how to do life. We are confident if we just get that next promotion or the next big bonus, then we have figured it out. And if we have it figured out, we will be happy. We say, "If I could just get to the next level, I'll be right where I need to be." If this is the correct attitude, will you ever be happy?

I lived the dream so many young baseball players have. I was a first-round pick, played in the Major Leagues, and became a multi-millionaire. Why couldn't I be happy? What was I missing? I lived my life based on the next goal, the next promotion, and the next contract. I wanted it so much, I neglected everything else, and my happiness was based on how I pitched that day. There is a better way to live. I never once took in the moment and enjoyed the moment of success.

Life is one giant unexpected event after another. Good events and bad events. In life, we never know what is going to happen day to day. I am a person, like many people, who does not like change. I thrive in a constant, consistent environment. Professional baseball is everything but consistent. The lack of control made me insane and frustrated. One day my arm would feel great; the next would be different. One game would go how I expected; the next game would go the completely opposite way. The structure was good for me, but change, not so much. What do we control in our lives?

If our life plan doesn't go how we want it to go, how do we respond? I had never quit anything or let something beat me. I believed I had control of my career until my elbow snapped three years into my career. This was the first traumatic experience that I had to overcome, and it became a defining moment for the rest of my life. It broke me. It broke my spirit, my self-respect, and my value. I was defeated because of my perception of failure. My question was "What do I do now and does it matter?"

This book is what I've learned about how to set goals, make good choices, and live a balanced life. We will discuss what it means to succeed and what it is that defines who you are. That's the process of Perspective, Perception, and Perseverance.

THE DEVELOPMENT OF MY PERSONALITY

I was born in Orange, Texas, on January 30, 1978. I am the son of Doug and Cheryl Patterson, and I have an older brother, Stephen, and a younger sister, Rebecca. Orange is a small east Texas town on the Texas/Louisiana border about ninety miles east of Houston on Interstate 10. The main industries of the area are chemical refineries, timber, and oil. Not much goes on in Orange but high school sports. The high schools are the pride and joy of most households, and bragging rights are golden. Fridays in the fall start at the football games and finish at Whataburger. It's a way of life.

Growing up in Orange meant that I would go to West Orange-Stark High School. It was the most successful athletic department in the area, if not the state, for its size. Like most small towns in Texas, football ruled, but baseball and basketball were not very far behind. My six-year older brother played football. I was so proud of him I wore his jersey to every game. The Mighty Mustangs, as they are known, had won two consecutive state championships in 1986 and 1987. I loved the feeling of being a part of a winning program. We walked a little taller and had a pride that others didn't. It motivated us, the younger generation, to continue the winning legacy that had been built before us. I think this is where I got my will to succeed and my work ethic. It was demanded.

My father was a professional baseball player with the Baltimore Orioles, and I had heard stories growing up about what an amazing athlete he was. I wanted to be like him and have people tell stories about me the way they talked about him. With his jet black hair and blue eyes, he looked like Superman. He was my idol. It just seemed that sports was a natural thing for me to go into. I played baseball, soccer, football, basketball and golf in middle school. When I reached high school I decided to play baseball only. I loved soccer, but baseball was in my blood, and it was what my family knew. When I decided at nine years old that I wanted to be a professional baseball player, my dad said, "Okay, we've got work to do."

And work is what we did. We would go to the youth fields of Orange, Texas, and work at Memorial Field. Not on skills, but actual work. We would mow, rake the infield, and paint what needed to be shined up. It was fun, hard, and hot, but fun. It taught me at a very young age that there was more to the game than just throwing and hitting the ball. When we were done, we would hit, throw, and take ground balls. He taught me the game, what it meant to be a baseball player, respect all aspects of the game, and to put in the time to get better. The best part came when we were done. We got a really good snow cone. We sat on the tailgate of his old truck and talked about our day, baseball, and the future. It was amazing to be with him and have quality time together.

When I was just shy of turning fourteen, my high school coach called me and invited me to come and throw for the Atlanta Braves scout at a tryout camp that was being held at the high school. I wasn't quite old enough yet, so I hadn't considered going. I called my parents and told them what happened, and they agreed to take me. I did not know what to expect and really had no expectations of how the day would go. I filled out my information card and designated myself as a shortstop and pitcher. We ran the sixty-yard dash first, and I ran somewhere around a 7.5-second sprint. It's really kind of funny now, but shortstops run a whole lot faster than that. Any time above seven seconds is not fast. Pitching was definitely more in my future. For about the next hour and a half, I just sat and waited on my turn to pitch. Being the young guy at the camp, I went last. I watched all of the older pitchers throw, and the whole time I said to myself, "I can do better than that." I just believed it. I threw eighty-one mph that day and threw some really nice, sharp curveballs. I could hear the buzz around the ballpark of people talking. When we were done, the scout came over and talked to the group of about thirty-five to forty players, and the only one he addressed was me. He said "Patterson, I will be back to see you!" I almost lost my mind. Did that really just happen? I could not wait to tell my parents. The Atlanta Braves were going to watch me play! We were so excited. It was beginning.

I had begun to attract attention from select travel teams all over the state. We felt that I had outgrown Orange and needed to face better competition and get more exposure. My dad would get calls from different teams and talk to coaches, but he never mentioned it to me. He would sort through all of the offers, and when he figured out the best place for me, he would ask me if I wanted to play. I always said, "Yes, let's do it." If I wanted to be the best, I needed to play the best.

My parents were hardworking people. My father worked for Chevron Chemical after his baseball career ended, and my mom was a teacher. We never felt poor but weren't rich. This was a big step for all of us. I respected them and wanted to have them be proud of me. I needed to be disciplined and not mess up my opportunity to step out and follow my dream. On Saturday mornings, my dad and I would leave our house at 5:30 to 6:00 a.m. to start the 1.5-hour drive to Houston. Two guys from a small town in Texas chasing a big league dream. I was starting to believe that I was in control of my fate. I had the talent, the guidance, and the family support to achieve my goals. We were laser focused, and that commitment paid off as we watched my baseball career prospects begin to skyrocket.

My sophomore year was my first year on the varsity team. More and more scouts began to fill the stands. They were starting to follow me every time I pitched. My velocity was increasing to around ninety mph, and I was gaining confidence at a rapid pace. My work ethic improved, and my focus was sharpening. I was living it on a daily basis, and baseball was all I could think about. Well, that and girls, but mostly baseball. I had stars in my eyes. I could not wait to get on the mound and strike someone, anyone, out. I had a poster on my ceiling above my bed of Nolan Ryan. He was the man, especially if you were a young pitcher from Texas. I went to sleep and woke up looking up to Nolan Ryan. I wanted from that moment on to be the next star first round pick from Texas. Tall, hard-throwing righty with a nasty curveball from the great state of Texas!

My junior year was a year that moved me into the top of my draft class. My velocity increased to ninety-four to ninety-five mph, and it separated me from almost everyone else. I was 6'4" and 165 pounds. Tall and lean. After the high school season, we decided for me to move six hours away from home to Dallas and play for the Dallas Mustangs who had recruited me. They were the best team in the state, if not the country, and it was a huge honor. It put financial stress on my family, but it was the right decision for my career. It was the first time I was away from my parents for an extended time period. It was a test in so many ways. I was living with my Aunt Jan, but I had to take care of myself and drive all over Dallas/Fort Worth to my games. I needed to get myself to the gym and take care of my diet. I was seventeen years old, testing to see if I could take care of myself. I did really well pitching and had a great time with my teammates, but failed miserably at taking care of myself. All I did was eat, play baseball, sleep, and do it over again. There was no balance. It was the most fun I had playing baseball and we won the Connie Mack World Series in Farmington, New Mexico. That's the best tournament you could win as a seventeen- to eighteen-year-old. At that point, I could pick whatever college program I wanted to go to. LSU, Miami, Arizona State, Texas, or TCU. I chose LSU. They were the number one team in the country and only two and a half hours from my hometown. We were hitting all of the milestones that we had dreamed of years before.

My senior year was all about the Major League Baseball Draft. My dream from the time I was nine years old was to be a first-round pick and play professional baseball. That had not changed, but I had narrowed it to I wanted to be the number one high school player in the country. Shoot high and I just might hit it. The first game I pitched that year had eighty-six scouts, cross checkers, and many Major League general managers there. It was comical to see. They filled up all of the bleachers behind home plate. As I would start to deliver a pitch, all you could see were radar guns raise to see how hard I was throwing. I never took it as pressure. It's exactly what I wanted. I was throwing up to ninety-eight mph and striking out two batters an inning. By the middle of the season, I knew I would be a top five pick. That is truly amazing to say, even today after all this time. As the season was winding down, I was one of two pitchers being considered for the number one overall pick. Kris Benson was the best college pitcher, and I was the best high school pitcher in the country. Seriously, if you had told that nine-year-old sitting in the driveway nine years earlier that he would be considered to be the first overall pick in the draft, his head would have exploded. But it was true, and it was happening.

Draft day June 4, 1996, was the most relaxed and yet anxious day of my life. We were about to find out where my future was. The local news crew trucks were parked outside, and close family members and friends were at my house waiting on the phone to ring. Fifteen minutes before the draft was to begin, the phone rang and everyone got extremely quiet to hear the news. It was Pittsburgh. They were calling to tell me that they had decided to go with Benson as the number one overall pick. They believed he was closer to being big-league ready because he was older and coming out of college. I was somewhat disappointed, but I understood, and it made some sense. Well, now where would I go? Five minutes later, the phone rang, and it was the Montreal Expos explaining that they had selected me with the fifth overall pick. I was so relieved and excited. We had done it. All of us. My family had done it. We all hugged, cried, and celebrated. All of the hard work, travel, money, blood, sweat, and tears had accomplished our goal.

If the story stopped right here, my life would have been perfect. What more could we possibly have accomplished? I was a first team All American, Gatorade Player of the Year, the fifth overall pick in the Major League Draft, and the first high school player drafted. I was happy and my family was proud of me. Most importantly, my dad was proud of me, and we had lived a father-and-son dream together. The American Dream. This is where it all goes crazy! Be careful what you wish for because you just might get it. All I wanted to do was play baseball.

Changing History

The summer Olympics were in Atlanta in 1996. That's important because the four picks in front of me were college players. Professional players did not play in the Olympics until the year 2000. It was amateur only in 1996. So, the four college players were on the Olympics team, and that meant they would not be negotiating their contracts until after they were finished playing. That was not a good situation for me. I wanted to go play, but I couldn't negotiate without knowing the financial numbers in front of me. All summer I waited. I mowed yards and tried to stay out of trouble. Montreal had made me a low offer, but it was not realistic. They were not interested in any negotiations. Now what? LSU started in August around the same time the Olympics ended. Should I go to school or maybe go to a junior college and enter the draft again? There were no good options. I was stuck.

In September, I got a call from my agent asking if I had received a letter from Montreal after the draft. My dad looked through all of his papers he had saved and could not find anything from them. Turns out, there was a rule that had been added to the draft that year. It said that every team had to send a formal written letter to every player drafted with an offer within two weeks of the draft day. Well, I never got one. Along with four other players in the first round, we had to make a major decision. File a complaint with Major League Baseball to gain free agency and risk everything or go to school. We chose to file a complaint.

Within a few weeks, we got a response that we were going to be granted free agency. Unbelievable. Before the draft, I wanted to break the high school record signing bonus of $1,600,000. It had been set a few years earlier by Josh Booty. Benson had signed for $2 million after the Olympics, so it was not unreasonable. Montreal just was not going to go that high. After I became a free agent, the offers started at $3 million, then $4 million. It was truly amazing to see what was happening. It was free-market capitalism at its finest! I was the same guy, but now worth two and three times as much. I traveled the country to the teams with the best offers, the New York Yankees, Tampa Bay Devil Rays, and Arizona Diamondbacks. When the dust settled, I was an Arizona Diamondback for the price of $6,075,000. I was finally a professional baseball player.

This was an unprecedented event. It had not occurred to me how this would change my career or how other players would perceive me. We had changed the draft process forever. The financial compensation tripled and quadrupled over the next few years. Guys were giving false addresses, trying to not receive their letters. We had made a lot of players a whole lot richer, but it also put a tremendous amount of pressure on me. I was treated differently, and I had a target on my back. I had always been the underdog from a small town. Now, I was on top, and it was an uneasy feeling for me. My personality started to change.

When you reach your dream, what do you do next? Seems like an easy answer. You pursue success and excellence. You aim for the next wrung on the ladder of achievement, and you keep pushing forward toward the next goal.

The Minor Leagues

It seemed so straightforward, but despite the surreal moment of being drafted, I was lost. When I left to play, I didn't have my dad with me anymore. I didn't realize how much things would change when I didn't have the same support system that brought me to that moment. I didn't know how to ask for help. Here was the culmination of everything that I'd worked so hard for, and I didn't know what to do with it.

My first spring training was in March 1997 in Yuma, Arizona. The Diamondbacks were an expansion team in 1996 and did not have its spring training facilities in Tucson built until 1998. My parents dropped me off at the airport in Houston, and it was an emotional moment for all of us. I was excited but nervous, and I think they were nervous and sad. I felt like I was ready, but I was leaving a huge part of me behind. I felt like I needed to be strong and show them I could be an independent adult. They were my team and my support system. My dad is the most caring and loving person who had done whatever I needed my whole life. At the same time, he could be overbearing and controlling. I wanted some space, but he knew I needed his guidance and knowledge. He had been through the process of being a professional athlete. He was just as invested in my future as I was. I just needed him to back off a little bit. I was wrong. I should have brought him with me. I had enough money to take care of my family, and I needed him to be there, just like he had always been.

Have you ever felt like your failure would let everyone you love down? My dad and I would talk every night after games, and I was living my dreams, but I was lonely. Underneath it all, there was an immense pressure to succeed, to win. I felt like if I failed, I was going to let down my family. It wasn't just my dream anymore. There were people who believed in me, invested in me, and I carried the weight of their expectations as much as my own. It wasn't true, of course, but it was how I felt at the time. I couldn't voice this to anyone, so instead, I let the pressure continue to build and build.

My first season I played at the Single A level in South Bend, Indiana. It's quite a bit different than playing in high school or travel ball teams where everyone is your age. Now, I was playing guys who had graduated college or had already played a year of pro ball. There is so much to learn the first year. Pro ball is a business. The seasons are long, and the bus rides seem never ending. We were lucky if we had a peanut butter and jelly sandwich before games and pizza after. Learning to deal with all of the different personalities and egos is difficult and humorous at times. I learned pretty quickly that I was a target.

It was not what I had envisioned when I said I want to play professional baseball. Some of the stadiums were nice, and some were absolutely horrible. We were paid $850 a month for a six-month season. It was not glamorous or what I would describe as fun. It was a high-pressure grinder that would spit you out and never think twice about it. I still enjoyed pitching but really did not like the lifestyle. I needed guidance. Growing up, my dad would tell me do this, this, and this, and I could do it. Now that he wasn't there, I had no one to tell me how to do this, this, and this. I never had to think, just throw. I needed someone to trust, to tell me what I needed to do, but I didn't have that person. I was alone.

Despite the pressure and lack of guidance, I was moving up in the minor leagues. I was an All-Star two of my first three years and the number two prospect in the organization. I was getting by on talent and talent alone. In 1999, I started the Double A All-Star game and was selected to play for Team USA in the Pan American Games in Winnipeg, Canada. The Pan American Games was the qualifier for the 2000 Olympics in Australia. It was an incredible accomplishment to be one of four starting pitchers, including Mark Mulder, Brad Penny, and Ryan Anderson, to represent our country. It was a welcomed change from the dog days of the minor leagues. I was given the honor of pitching the opening game against Canada and the quarterfinal game against Panama. I carried a perfect game into the eighth inning before giving up a hit against Panama. All of my family was there to support me, and we ended up winning the silver medal after losing to Cuba in the gold medal game. Not winning the gold was difficult, but we had qualified for the Olympics the following year. It was an unbelievable experience to represent the United States that I will always cherish.

After the games were over, I was moved from Double A to Triple A, one level below the Major Leagues. I was getting very close to achieving my goal of being twenty-one years old in the big leagues. I could taste it and was one step away from the next and biggest milestone of my life. At this level, I just needed to stay healthy and show some consistency. It was a challenge facing older, more experienced hitters. I pitched okay, but not great. I felt average at best, but I was tired. It had been an emotional and long year. My body was really feeling the stress.

My last start of the year came at the end of August, and all of the Arizona Diamondbacks executives were there to see me pitch. It was so unbelievable; I was about to get called up to the Major Leagues for September. As I was warming up for the game, I felt a pop in my rib cage. It hurt badly and was extremely hard to continue to throw. I knew it was not good.

The first inning started, and I could hardly throw. I'm not sure I even got anyone out and had to be removed from the game. I had torn an abdominal muscle. That one pop had changed the rest of my life. The minor league pitching coordinator came into the training room to check on me and to tell me that they couldn't call me up since I was hurt. Devastated would be an understatement. I was probably one hour or so away from achieving everything I had worked my whole life for, and it was gone in an instant. I had to sit at my locker and watch my friends and teammates get good news, pack their bags, and head to Phoenix as Major Leaguers.

What do you do when all of your carefully laid plans are derailed by something you never could have anticipated? I had dealt with injuries before, but not being called up at twenty-one rattled me mentally. I should have spoken up about how devastated I was. It was one of those things in life that meant more than others. This was my last goal to reach what I thought was success. My mental health was starting to break at this point of my career.

Self-Medicating

The fall of 1999, I was playing in the Arizona Fall League, and it can be described as a top prospect league for future Major League players. I was very distracted by mostly everything. Baseball was not where my focus was. This was the first time I smoked marijuana regularly, daily. We would play our game, head back to the apartment, smoke, and play video games. I don't even like video games, but it was relaxing, an escape from stress and pain that I felt in my body and arm. I had noticed throughout the year that my velocity had gone down. The year before, I averaged ninety-four mph, topped out at one hundred mph and now, I was topping out at ninety-four. I could not throw in the upper nineties anymore. I was concerned, but not worried.

Weed was my way of checking out of reality, and maybe deep down, that was telling me something. I was not okay. I was subconsciously very disappointed and not equipped to talk about the disappointment. Had I failed? It felt like failure to me, for sure. It was the first time in my life I had not hit the milestone I set for myself. That should have been a confidence booster, but it had the opposite effect on me. My perspective was not correct. At the end of the Fall League, I was named the number ten prospect in all of baseball and the number one right-handed pitcher. That is a huge accomplishment, and I should have been happy, but I wasn't.

I looked at the injury not as a learning situation and motivation for the following year, but as I had failed to succeed. I forgot about all of the successes in my life and what I had to be thankful for. The downward spiral was starting to take shape. I had let myself down, my family down, the organization down, and I was at a complete loss on how to handle the disappointment.

The Final Nail

I thought I'd successfully turned my injury around. I had a really good off-season, and my arm was loose and pain free. It was going to be an amazing year. I was either going to be in the big leagues or I was going to be playing in the Olympics during the summer. A big leaguer and/or an Olympian. It doesn't get better than that.

Spring training started, and I was receiving attention from the coaches and media. It really felt like the spot available in the rotation was mine to lose. I was confident in my ability, but I still was not comfortable with the older players. Randy Johnson, Curt Schilling, Matt Williams, Luis Gonzalez, Mark Grace, Greg Swindell, and Steve Finley were all players I grew up watching on television. These guys were baseball royalty. I had earned some of their respect, but they still weren't sure about me. I was shy and reclusive. I was always described as having a "quiet confidence." Some people took it as arrogance because of how the draft had gone years earlier, but it wasn't.

I was waiting to show them I could pitch, and I believed that would break the ice for us to have a relationship. I believed my value was in my ability to pitch, not in my friendship.

In my second game of the spring, I noticed I just didn't have any velocity, and my breaking balls were not sharp. My arm was stiff, and I could hardly move it. Washing my hair was painful and driving with my arm on the center armrest was making my arm go numb. My pitching coach had a conversation with me about the velocity drop, and I assured him it would get better. But would it, I wondered. I had never felt anything like it, and I could not straighten my arm. I got demoted to minor league camp with the promise that when my arm was better, I would be called back up. More disappointment and no answers to be had.

My first MRI was somewhat positive, and I received cortisone injections, rest, and a chance to breathe. I told myself this would fix my issue and I'd be back in two weeks. Well, I was back in two weeks, but I was probably worse than before. Pain would be an understatement, and I really had no business being on the field. My second MRI was the last nail in the coffin for John Patterson. I had no ligament left in my elbow and would need Tommy John surgery. Ligament replacement surgery is an eighteen- to twenty-four-month recovery time process. I was numb. I could not cry, talk, or drive my car home. It was a blur and I had to have my girlfriend drive me home. That was the day John Patterson 1.0 died. Setback after setback, while still maintaining the heavy burden of pressure, was all too much to bear.

My surgery was performed by Dr. James Andrews in Birmingham, Alabama. The night before the operation, I sat in my parents' hotel room, sad and depressed. They were trying to console me, but I said, "If I come out of this surgery different, I don't want to play anymore." I had always prided myself on throwing hard and striking batters out. If I was not going to be able to be that type of pitcher, I didn't want to pitch. That statement was a defining moment for the next three years.

I was at my lowest point and began using pain pills on top of smoking weed. This helped me escape and numb my body and emotions. Then I started mixing in the alcohol, and this helped curb my anxiety and gave me the false feeling that I was okay and could face people. Once this wasn't enough to kill the mental and physical pain, it escalated to using ecstasy and eventually cocaine. I quit talking to my family, pulling myself even further away from what had always been my strongest base of support. Depression was setting in, and I was acting like nothing was wrong. It was a front to the world. I'm great, don't worry about me. The drugs increased, and I had no energy to face my depression.

In my mind, I was a complete failure. It was over. No more dreams or goals. Just me, my girlfriend, my dogs, and a really dark apartment, getting high as possible. I would watch games on TV, but I'm not sure why. I was beginning to despise baseball, the game that had given me so much joy and happiness. The game that had built my parents a beautiful house when I was twenty years old. The game that paid for my mom's BMW and my sister's college tuition, helped my brother and paid off the debt my parents accrued getting me to this point. I also felt embarrassed to have this much money and felt it was my responsibility to pay for everything for them. I wanted to repay them for all the sacrifices they made for me. Sharing the wealth with them felt like it was what I supposed to do.

I had been able to do so much for my family because of baseball, but I couldn't see it all. I could only see the failure and not achieving the goal I focused so much of my attention on since I was nine, that is, being in the big leagues at twenty-one years old. I didn't want to play anymore. I was damaging myself and my mind daily and without regard for the future. If I died, so be it. Nothing mattered anymore, least of all me.

Chapter 1

SUCCESS AND FAILURE

How do you define success?

The Merriam-Webster definition of success is (1) obsolete outcome, result; (2) degree or measure of succeeding; (3) favorable or desired outcome; (4) the attainment of wealth, favor, or eminence; (5) one that succeeds.

The words that jump out at me are *desired outcome*. I believe most people would agree that their desired outcome would be wealth, fame, and having their dream come true. Success, for me, was being in the Major Leagues by the time I was twenty-one. I wanted to be twenty-one, throwing one hundred mph and striking out the best hitters in the world. In baseball, there is an attraction to having the young pitcher who throws exceptionally hard. Management and the media are drawn to it like a moth to a flame. The older you get, the less attractive it is. I knew that. If I was able to accomplish that goal, the rest of things I wanted would follow and the pressure would lessen, to a degree. I had achieved all of my goals I had set for myself, and this was the last goal on my list. It did not seem like an unreasonable idea, considering my accomplishments to that point in my life. That's it. My only definition of success.

Success is an idea that we make up in our head. I'd always thought about success in terms of milestones. Where I was supposed to be: in baseball, my career, and my personal relationships. The problem with this way of thinking is that life is short, and the unexpected can and does happen. If I wasn't meeting certain milestones at a certain age, at a certain time of being inside the professional game, surely I was falling behind at my definition of success in life. And so, I put an extreme amount of pressure on myself that if I didn't meet those milestones, I was failing.

Having a goal and an idea of where you want to be in the future is a good thing, but saying it and understanding how to get there are two different things. Success could be described as learning and failure as not learning and improving. Success comes when you combine all of the things you have learned from life experiences. Success is not just the next item of the day; it is the day. You are alive, and you need to be grateful for all of your gifts. I was not present and enjoying every day like I should have been because I was focused on the wrong ideas. Success is not money or status. Failure is not a setback or a mistake. Success is hard to come by, and you must enjoy what you are doing, or you will feel failure where it is not. Success is not guaranteed, but failure is. How you respond to a setback or a fork in the road is the second most important lesson in life you can learn. The first is God has a plan for you!

> *"Success is liking yourself, liking what you do,*
> *and liking how you do it."*
> **MAYA ANGELOU**

I think a lot of people that are ambitious, or grew up in a very successful family that maybe had successful brothers, sisters, parents, and so on. tend to think in terms of milestones too. You're "supposed" to graduate college by twenty-two, have a solid job by twenty-four, hold X position in a company, drive a certain kind of car, buy a house by thirty, the list goes on and on. If for whatever reason things don't turn out that way, then you feel like you're failing.

Having the right mind-set to succeed is often overlooked. Your mind-set is believing that you can accomplish your goal, but understanding you will have bumps in the road along the way. Staying positive and making adjustments as you go will be necessary. In our youth, we often believe the path to success is a straight line. For some people it might be, but for most of us it is a roller coaster. That roller coaster teaches you how to navigate through life's ups and downs.

There is a process to gaining success. Success has so many variables from person to person. Some people just want a wealth of happiness, and others want wealth. What would be your wealth of happiness? Knowing what makes you happy is you going through the process of achieving wealth of happiness. If you just want wealth, can you be happy? What would be enough? If you don't enjoy what you are doing but make millions of dollars, are you successful? I was doing exactly what I had always wanted to do, but I wasn't happy. My daily routine was not fun, and I didn't enjoy it. I didn't feel successful.

To be successful, you enjoy the ride of life. Set goals and enjoy the ups and downs. It won't be perfect, and it will be painful at times, but get on the train to happiness. Life isn't perfect. Enjoy every day and put people around you that lift you up. It won't go how you want it to go all the time, but don't sacrifice who you are. You deserve to be happy. Set goals, be a good person, and always strive to be better.

> *"Becoming a champion is not an easy process ...*
> *It is done by focusing on what it takes to get*
> *there and not on getting there."*
> **NICK SABAN**

I remember another ballplayer who had a similar surgery to mine, and to look at him you wouldn't know that he was going through extensive physical rehab. He went about his treatment like it was a normal day. Why was he able to do that, and I was not?

What I realized is it has everything to do with mind-set. He was able to take a realistic look at his situation and set reasonable expectations for himself and his progress. I was looking backward at what I had lost, and he was looking forward to where he was going. I couldn't get over the fact I wasn't going to play baseball for at least twelve months and that my dream was over. He looked at it as the next challenge and that everything would work out fine. Not failure, just the next obstacle of the day. When I had my surgery and did not accomplish my ultimate goal, I felt true loss for the first time. My mind-set changed from "I can do it" to "I don't care." My idea of success was gone. I believed I failed based on the idea I had not reached a milestone I had rigidly set for myself. I needed to be grateful and trust that God had my back.

Does your plan for success include unexpected setbacks? Success and failure go hand in hand. It will happen, and you should be ready to react in a healthy way. The most success-ful people have failed more times than they have succeeded. Successful people look for the right perspective. Perspective is so important to living a healthy and happy life. The right perspective of your blessings and place in life at the current time gives you the strength to fight on. Fight for your new goals. Fight for your career, your family, and yourself. You are successful if you can find the right perspective.

When you are a goal-driven person like I was, there's con-stantly a question of "what's next." When I achieved a goal, there was never any time to savor it. I would be glad I achieved that milestone, but I couldn't help worrying about the next step; that was how I kept motivated. This was my failure. It was not the injury, but that I didn't focus on the gifts God had given to me and be grateful. My perspective was all wrong. I felt sorry for myself, and I changed my life in a way I never could have expected.

When something bad has happened, many people's first instinct is to ask, "Why me? How could this happen to me?" The questions aren't "why" or "how," the question is what will you do going forward?

What about having a traumatic event in your life? In my case, it was injury. It other cases, it could be a car wreck, a job layoff, or a death in the family, anything that you did not see coming that changes the direction or timing of your life.

So what do you do when your life takes an unexpected turn that causes you pain? In my experience, it's not dissimilar from the Kübler-Ross stages of grief: denial, anger, bargaining, de-pression, and acceptance. Not everyone experiences them in the same order and not in the same way.

Some people overeat, overdrink, or overthink. Numbing emotions is a common way to overcome stress, and I had mastered that. When something tragic happens, our first instinct is usually to retreat or be destructive. We tell ourselves it's our fault, right or wrong. We try to make ourselves feel better with substances, sleeping all day, or surrounding ourselves with people who tell us what we want to hear. We ultimately don't make the situation any better. We complicate the matter by trying to control that situation.

A better solution is to take one day at a time, and pause.

Accept the situation, allow yourself to grieve, and tell yourself that you will become stronger because of it. That is all that we can control. No matter what you're going through, know that everyone experiences the same ups and downs. Life doesn't let anyone out unscathed. You are the master of your responses to the unexpected, so why not manage your emotions now? Don't wait for the unexpected to occur. Practice preparing yourself to manage the hard times as well as you do the easy ones. Get yourself a team of people who will support you and remember that you are never alone, and you will get through anything that's put in your path.

Failure is an interesting word to me. Our society almost makes it seem like failure is the end. It's in the way we're programmed. Failure has come to mean that there isn't anything worthwhile on the rest of our journeys. This couldn't be further from the truth. The goal is to take those lessons and apply them to everything you do thereafter. Learn, grow, and keep reaching upward toward your goal.

Chapter 2

PERSEVERANCE

Have you ever been in a position where it felt like you had nothing going for you but frustration and anxiety? Sometimes that season of waiting for success or the next step can feel like an empty desert. Maybe you have to pivot and try something new, or maybe it's taking more time than you thought to achieve your goals. You may not even have any idea how you got to where you currently are.

When I was twenty-two to twenty-three years old, I asked myself repeatedly if I even wanted to play baseball anymore. My perspective of where I was in my life was all wrong. My perception of myself was even worse. But the one thing I did have was perseverance. Something inside of me would not let me quit. I kept working, although some days better than others. I was struggling with addiction and depression, but I was pushing myself forward. Deep down, I still believed I could play in the big leagues, and I wanted know what it felt like to stand on a Major League mound.

During the summer of 2002, I was starting to make progress in my recovery physically. I was getting my velocity back and beginning to believe I could pitch again. I was in Tucson, Arizona, at the Triple A level, having a solid year. I needed something to go my way, just one thing to break my way and I would get my call to the Major Leagues. On July 18, I got the call I had waited my entire life for. We were in Sacramento, California, and the hotel phone rang early in the morning. I woke up, picked up the phone, and just hung it back up, thinking it was a wakeup call. Again the phone rang, and I hung it back up. A few minutes later, my cell phone rang, and I could see it was an Arizona number. I answered and it was Tommy Jones, the minor league coordinator. He said, "Hello John, have you ever been to San Diego?" I said "No" as I rubbed my eyes. He replied, "Well, pack your bags because you are pitching against the San Diego Padres on Saturday night!" There it was. I jumped up out of that bed like I had been electrocuted. It was pure joy, and I could not thank him enough for the opportunity. In that moment, my perspective changed instantly. I was no longer a failure, I was a success.

It takes perseverance and time to progress toward your dream. I had spent years of my life driving to rehab my arm and back to my apartment. Where was my life going? How do I move forward? It was a slow process that had no end in sight. But I kept going. I was progressing even when I didn't recognize it because I was persevering.

Perseverance brings you joy because when you succeed, you look back at all of the obstacles you overcame. You got stronger. Your faith in yourself and God became greater. Your dreams became a reality. You cannot achieve anything dwelling on the past or wondering "what if." Fight forward and focus on all of the good things coming your way, if you just keep persevering.

When I got off of the phone with Tommy, I needed to call my parents, and let them know the good news. How would

I tell them, I wondered? I called their house, and my mom answered. "Hi Momma. How are you? Is Daddy there?" "No, he is at work," she said. I asked, "Can you call and ask him to come home?" "Sure, I'll call you when he gets here." It felt like forever. I couldn't wait to tell them. Thirty minutes later, they called back, and I asked them if they had ever been to the San Diego Zoo. "No, why?" "Because I am going to be pitching against the Padres on Saturday night!" We were so excited that it had finally happened. All of the pain seemed to go away in that moment. The years of fighting with my dad, avoiding phone calls, and depression from my sense of failure went away. I had brought them joy again, and it felt amazing. Everything felt possible again because we had persevered through the pain.

We will not always know why our lives hit roadblocks or change course. Other times, we will know exactly where we went wrong or what happened. Perseverance, pushing through, never quitting, and making the tough decisions to get better, gives us the ability to change the direction of our lives.

On July 20, 2002, I made my Major League debut. My whole family and our closest friends had made the trip to California. It was a beautiful Southern California night with fifty-five thousand people in attendance. I was nervous but focused. As I made my way to the mound, my legs were a little wobbly, and my heart was racing. Every part of my life had led me to this moment. My body was numb, but my mind was sharp. I started my delivery and threw a perfect fastball over the outside corner for strike one on my first pitch. Now, I could breathe for the first time all night. The noise, the smell of the ballpark, and the electricity in the air were amazing. I struck out the second batter I faced, Mark Kotsay, on a curveball and then I'm fairly sure I blacked out because I don't remember anything else until the seventh inning.

I can remember sitting in the dugout, listening to the seventh inning stretch song "Take Me Out to the Ball Game" and scanning the stands. Seeing all of the fans there was breathtaking. I finished the night pitching six innings, giving up one run, and getting a no decision, but it was incredible. After the game, I went out onto the field, and looked at the empty stadium one more time. It was a moment I didn't want to end. My dad had given me a small canister to bring him some of the dirt from the mound as a souvenir. I scooped some of it up and screwed the lid on tight. I wanted to preserve this day for him and me. I walked out of the stadium to meet all of my family and friends for the first time as a Major League Baseball player.

I had broken through the negative and started thinking positive again. I felt as though I was a new person. The pressure and stress that we put on ourselves builds and builds until something gives. Our lack of patience can make us do things completely out of our personality because we want to achieve our goals immediately. Instead of looking at roadblocks to our goals as failures, let's look at them as character-building blocks. Your perseverance through these times builds character. It becomes a way that you can define yourself. We all know quitters, and we also know people that refuse to lose. Who would you rather be?

My wife is one of the most competitive people I know. She works until she is exhausted, and then she works some more. She will come tell me how she is "burnt out" and then go back into her office and work some more. She refuses to let herself not persevere. She is successful, and everyone who knows her comments on the fact she does not quit. Ever. This is how you succeed. Never give up. Make adjustments, but never give up.

I learned an exercise years ago that has helped me tremendously. Whenever something or somebody is bringing you down, write a letter. I was having a huge problem letting go of the "what ifs" in my life, specifically, my first elbow surgery. The therapist I was working with at the time told me to sit down and write a letter to my elbow. Write down all of the thoughts I had about my elbow, good and bad. I thought about it for a few days, procrastinated a few more days, and then started writing. The words were flowing out of me like I couldn't believe.

I was angry at it because it had given out on me when I needed it the most. But, that's not what I was writing. Instead, I was writing a thank-you note. How could this be? It was because I was grateful to my elbow getting me to my dream, not that it had let me down. It had not let me down. Everything I have is, in part, because of my elbow. My career and my relationships with my family, my wife, and my son are all because of my elbow. My elbow had taught me a valuable lesson, perseverance. It taught me how to fight forward and the victory at the end will be that much sweeter. I would encourage you to write a letter to whatever it is that is holding you back. You might be surprised by what happens.

When I was growing up in Orange, perseverance was what drove me. Growing up in a small town has some advantages and some drawbacks. Everyone knows everyone. There is a desire for people to be the same. If you get outside of the norm, you set yourself apart. People attacked me for wanting to be different. I didn't want to work at the chemical refinery or be a high school baseball coach. I didn't think I was better than anyone else, but I didn't want the same things. I did not want to stay in Orange. I wanted to be a baseball player at the highest level. Teammates, coaches, and so-called friends came after me and my family with, "Who do you think you are?" The high school coaches wanted me to play with my high school teammates during the summer, and my teammates did not seem to like me separating myself from them. The only way for me to survive was to persevere. My personality began to change, and my mindset became "I will prove you wrong because this is the best opportunity for me to excel."

I had a teacher who would come and watch me practice after school. She would stand in the alleyway and watch my dad and me work on all parts of my game for hours, every day. One day, she came to me and asked, "Does your dad force you to play baseball?" I was a shocked she would ask me that. "No," I answered. "I enjoy it." She couldn't believe that I wanted to train that much. She came back to me another day and told me she was willing to fail me so I wouldn't have to play. She couldn't wrap her mind around me loving the game that much. She wasn't the only teacher that thought that, but she was the only one who ever asked me. I had coaches who attacked me because I was a distraction to the team. I was getting so much attention that they couldn't control me like they could everyone else. I had dealt with coaches before, but it was getting abusive. I developed a huge mistrust of coaches and teachers that would eventually show itself once I was in pro ball. I didn't look at these people as helpers; I looked at them with spite and mistrust.

My senior year, we played a game against our district rival, Little Cypress-Mauriceville. It was always a competitive game, but this one was one for the history books. I had already signed with LSU, and the opposing pitcher was a junior who eventually went to the University of Texas. It was standing room only, and the stands were packed with scouts. That week, I had been featured on ESPN and Fox Sports, and it was a circus atmosphere all week leading up to the game. I had never seen adults act as aggressively toward us as they did that week. Imagine parents wanting to watch their child play being pushed out of the stands by scouts.

I had a perfect game going until the sixth inning and hung a slider that was hit out of the ballpark for a home run. The opposing fans went nuts. They were chanting "LSU, LSU, LSU" to mock me, but I kept my composure. In my mind, I was thinking more like "first round, first round, first round draft pick," but whatever. We ended up losing the game 1-0. After the game, people were literally trying to attack me and my family. We had to all group together and be surrounded by my team and fans to be walked to the bus. It was crazy. Years later, when I was in pro ball, I had scouts come up to me, who had been at that game and tell me it was one of the best high school games they had ever seen.

My point in telling you this is when you step out to chase your dreams, you are going to lose friends, and you will draw attention to yourself. As painful as it was for us, we knew we were doing the right thing for me. I think it was a defining moment in my childhood. It made me calloused to everyone and everything around me. I was fighting teachers, coaches, and teammates, and then having to face opposing teams. I could only trust my family and persevere the best way I knew how. I focused on my goals and my goals only. It was the fuel I needed to continue to survive. Find what drives you and use it.

Perseverance makes us tough. It makes us do things we did not know we could do. Saying you want to do something and doing it is hard. That's where perseverance comes in. People told me I would not be a first-round draft pick. People told me I would not be a Major League pitcher. Nobody believed I would put my career back together. People didn't believe I would be an opening-day starter. They were all wrong.

On a more personal level, my wife and I struggled to have a baby. From the time we were engaged, we had discussed wanting to get pregnant immediately after being married. My career had just ended, and I wanted more than anything to have a son. At the time, I didn't feel as though I was trying to fill a void in my life, but looking back, I most likely was. We tried over and over, with no luck. Anyone who has tried to plan a baby knows how it can become a chore and everything is on a schedule. We were at a loss, trying to figure out how to make our desire of having a baby come true. As the years passed, we began to wonder if having a child was even possible. Shannon visited with doctor after doctor to try and receive answers to our questions.

After we moved to the Dallas, Texas, area, she met with another doctor. After meeting with us for thirty minutes, we could tell something was different. She had additional tests run and referred us to an infertility specialist. It was then determined Shannon had a heart-shaped uterus, endometriosis, and we had a 0 percent chance of getting pregnant on our own. We had to have a surgery to correct the heart-shaped uterus and remove the endometriosis. Our doctor wanted to start the in vitro fertilization (IVF) immediately, but Shannon wasn't emotionally ready. It was difficult situation, and it put a tremendous amount of stress on our marriage. I wanted a baby, and she was dealing with depression and sadness from not being able to get pregnant. We were not able to communicate in a healthy way about how broken and hopeless we felt. It took a few more years and seeing a counselor to help us both heal and gain the strength to continue to try.

Because so much time had passed, Shannon's endometriosis had returned, and we needed to have another surgery before attempting the IVF process. So, after eight years of trying to have a baby on our own, we made it to the IVF process. We did it a little bit differently and spread out the process over seven months. We were cautious and didn't want to push Shannon's body. On January 13, 2016, we did the transfer of the embryo and the stress of hoping it would "take" began. We had multiple episodes of fear over the next three months. The worst was the day before we were scheduled to hear the baby's heartbeat for the first time. Shannon broke out in a rash and hives because of an allergic reaction to the shots I had to give her. We didn't know the cause and feared for the worst as we rushed to the doctor's office. Our doctor was noticeably concerned and ordered an ultrasound immediately. Within a matter of minutes, we went from one of the most terrifying moments of our life to the most joyous, when we heard our baby's heartbeat for the very first time. We cried tears of happiness for the first time in many years.

On September 25, 2016, Palmer Douglas Patterson was born at 10:10 a.m. Our miracle baby was finally in our arms. We had persevered for nine years. It would have been so easy to give up or have our relationship become unrecoverable because of the feelings of failure. It took us many years of hardship, recovery, and perseverance to make our miracle happen. Looking back now, we are so grateful that we did not give up.

When I woke up this morning, I had my two-and-a-half-year-old son lying next to me. The joy that he gives me and the smile on my wife's face when she watches us makes all of the pain and adversity worth it.

Chapter 3

THE EXPECTATION OF SETTING GOALS

Life is a series of course corrections, including the creation and recreation of setting goals for our family life and our professional life. So often, we begin to make these plans, and we forget that we need to be flexible to the patterns of life.

When I was in my teens, I would write down my goals for the upcoming season, usually ten to fifteen items I wanted to accomplish. I would make two copies, one for at home and one for my locker at school. I also shared these goals with my parents, and they helped hold me accountable and kept me on track. Every week, I would look it over and remind myself what I was working for. It would motivate me to work harder and make wiser decisions. It is the best way that I have found to make myself accountable. Without reminding yourself why you are doing what you are doing, you can spin out of control quickly. But, having an expectation of the desired outcome to be what you want is the wrong mindset. Setting goals is a tool, not a genie in a bottle.

In the present, I have returned to setting goals at the beginning of every year. With my maturity and growth, I have realized what I did in my teens was very short sighted and lead to my downfall. As I matured, I have realized the value in looking further into my future and that there is more to the process.

There are three types of goals: short-term, intermediate-term, and long-term. In the short term, your focus is your daily and weekly routine. Short-term goals keep you organized and healthy. They are attainable goals but still push you toward accomplishing your long-term goals. When I played baseball, it was watching videos, eating a healthy diet, working out, and reading. These were things I could block my day out for and control in my daily routine. My current life in real estate is developing plans for my next house, watching shows, and researching. These help me chip away at my long-term goals.

Your intermediate goals are your quarterly goals. They involve a scale of judgment. Am I where I thought I would be at this point in time? Where do I need to make an adjustment if I am not? I always analyzed if I needed to change my diet, add stretching, adjust my throwing program, or adjust my strategy.

The long term includes your yearly to multiyear goals. Long-term goals are the prize at the end if you maintained discipline and got a little lucky along the way. Every time I have used this formula, I have had successes. Nothing is 100 percent, but I had some great success in using this road map. Every time I did not use this formula, I became overwhelmed, lost the way, and made poor decisions. Sounds easy, right?

What is so hard about sitting down, writing goals for your future and your family's future, and staying focused on the process? The easy answer is nothing. The more complicated answer is the unexpected and the unforeseen events of life. If it was easy, everyone would be goal-setting overachievers. In reality, how many goal-setting overachievers do you know? The bigger the goal, the more you have to push yourself outside of your comfort zone.

It takes a huge amount of discipline and accountability for yourself and your family. This is not about perfection; it is about being the best you can be, pushing yourself further than you believed you can go. In doing this exercise, it is easy to go too far overboard. I should know; I'm an extremist. Everything I have done in my life that I truly care about, I do to the extreme.

After my first season in the big leagues, I decided that I would work twice as hard as I had ever worked before. For my long-term goals, for the next season, I wanted to be the number three starter behind Randy Johnson and Curt Schilling and be in the running for Rookie of the Year. This was a solid goal but not unreasonable. I had pitched really well the 2002 season, with a breakout start against the St. Louis Cardinals and pitched the final game of the year against the Colorado Rockies for home field advantage in the playoffs that we won. I had only gotten a taste of what it was like to be in the big leagues, pitching in seven games, starting five, and finishing with a record of 2-0 and 3.23 ERA. I was healthy, confident, and had made huge progress in my physical recovery. I had gained the confidence that I needed to have trust in the fact I could pitch at the highest level. As I mentioned earlier, I loved striking batters out. I had struck out Albert Pujols the first time I faced him. One of my idols growing up was Ken Griffey Jr., and I struck him out three times in a row the first times facing him. It was awesome. A dream come true.

My short-term goals included working out twice a day, mornings and evenings five days a week. I would get up early in the morning, have a balanced breakfast with a protein shake, and head to Bank One Ballpark in Phoenix to train with the Diamondbacks medical staff. I would lift weights, run, do my arm exercises, and throw with Schilling. After the morning workout, I would head back to my apartment to eat a high-protein lunch and take a nap. At around 5:00, I would load up on carbs and more protein, and head to a North Scottsdale gym to meet my personal trainer. We would work a different muscle group than the morning workout and train my abs. I then would drive home, eat as many calories as I could, and fall asleep. I would get up the next day and do it all over again, for four straight months.

My intermediate goals were to have a strong showing in spring training and have over half of my starts for the season be quality starts. A quality start is six innings or more, giving up three runs or less.

I had set the bar high, but I was motivated. I was putting all of my time into and making the sacrifices it takes to achieve at a high level. The problem was, I was exhausted. I never gave myself a chance to relax. The harder I worked, the more stressed I got. I was consumed with perfection. I wanted to look a certain way. I wanted 3 percent body fat and to weigh 220 pounds. I was accomplishing my goals, but I was just going way too hard. By the time Spring Training came around, I was mentally drained. I was running on adrenaline, but my body started breaking down.

The professional baseball season is seven and a half months long from the beginning of spring training in the middle of February to the end of September. There are 162 games in the regular season and around 40 games in Spring Training. We worked every day. If you make the playoffs, it runs through

October. It's a marathon. My being exhausted and breaking down so early in the year was a huge problem. I pitched well early in camp, but I was getting average results, and because of the fatigue, I got angry at myself. How could I have worked so hard and achieved all of my short-term goals, only to not see the benefit on the field now? Sometimes we just want it too badly.

I ended up being the last player cut from the roster on the last day of Spring Training. I had already moved to Phoenix from Tucson. I was called into the office the day before the season was to start and told I was going back to Triple A in Tucson. I couldn't believe it.

I drove back to Tucson and checked into a rent-by-the-week hotel room that was a complete dump. I did enough cocaine over the next week to kill a horse. I was emotionally devastated and wanted to be cut from the organization. Not making the roster had derailed me from my goals. When I re-calibrated, it was in an extremely unhealthy way, and I wanted to be traded. The whole season ended up being a merry-go-round. I would pitch well in Triple A and get called up. I would pitch a good game and then a bad game and get sent down. It was awful for my mental health. Even worse was I had made the same mistake I made after my surgery a few years before. I started trying to numb the pain of not achieving the goals I had set for myself. I was teetering on the edge. I needed a new environment and a fresh start. The success I was craving was not going to happen in Arizona.

Goals are a funny thing. They can be great and still not get you where you want to go. I needed to adjust and calm down. There is no room in success for perfection. I realized that I was not only looking for success by achieving my goals, but that I was looking for perfection. Change your expectation. Accomplishing goals and having the expectation of your expected outcome is dangerous. It won't work perfectly every day. Each day is new. That striving for perfection will leave you feeling hopeless. Instead, give yourself the space to realize that course corrections are normal and maintaining a positive mindset can be the determining factor to how you view yourself and your path forward. Readjust if you get too far behind. Don't allow it to overwhelm you. Maybe go back to the short-term goals and reset.

As I teach and work with kids, I try to be as positive as I possibly can. "Kids, you need to learn the phrase 'It's just baseball, and it's not going to be perfect.'" You are not going to have control over every aspect, every day. The sooner that you can learn the saying "It's just baseball," the quicker you'll learn to just let it go and come back the next day. If you don't hold on to that phrase, then eventually you'll start to beat yourself up. You will become consumed with negative self-talk. That is the exact opposite of what the game is about and what you're trying to accomplish. Soon, you will notice you have stopped making progress. This statement is true in all professions. Learn the phrase "It's just life."

Goals are meant to keep us positive. They are there to give us something to strive for, not to make us feel like failures. Our perception of what our goals are and why we are striving for them is our mind-set. Is it for a good reason or do we have the wrong intention? It's extremely easy to get so consumed with your goals that you lose sight of your "why" sometimes. This is when we need to recalibrate and gain a better perspective. In life, flying by the seat of your pants can be a good thing, but not for a long-term plan. Step back and reevaluate your goals.

The Perfect Pitch

I am often asked if there is such a thing as a perfect pitch. Yes! The perfect pitch is strike one. It could be a fastball, curveball, slider, or changeup. There isn't one perfect pitch. It is whatever the pitch is for strike one, even if the pitch wasn't truly perfect. For that moment, even if it was a little high, or it wasn't as fast as I wanted, for that moment, for that batter, it was perfect.

Imperfections can be perfect sometimes. I truly expected that I could throw the ball exactly where I wanted to every time. It isn't possible 100 percent of the time, but what about 95 percent of the time? It's a flaw, but it's also a motivator. If you don't have confidence in yourself, then nobody's going to have confidence in you or your abilities. It isn't a weakness until it starts to tear you down. When you feel like you're failing if you didn't do it perfectly, now it becomes a negative, not a positive. When I would pitch a good game and struck out eight or nine batters, many times I would go home mad. Why? I had done my job and done it well. After my surgery, I didn't throw as hard as I did before. In the back of my mind, I would be thinking that if I hadn't had the surgery and I still threw as hard as I did before, I would have struck out thirteen or fourteen. It was a flaw. My expectation needed to change.

Your skill, your talent, is so much bigger than perfection. I could throw every pitch where I wanted and still lose. But it could be that the game I didn't pitch perfectly was the one that brought the win. I can remember pitching so many great games and going home unhappy. I dwelled on the mistakes, and I couldn't get past the lack of perfection. Perfection is a cancer for your happiness. We can't be perfect. Only God is perfect. No matter how big our ego is, we are not God, so in return, we are not perfect. If we can accept that, we move forward and become happy by trying our hardest. It's all that we can control.

THINGS TO THINK ON:

- How can you change the way you view and manage seeking perfection?

- List the top five goals you have right now.

- What are your short and intermediate goals to help you get there?

- Is the lofty goal of perfection making you unhappy and preventing you from reaching them?

- Are you willing to adjust if obstacles start to get in the way of you reaching your goals?

Chapter 4

SAY IT OUT LOUD

The hardest thing to do is ask for help. It was for me. Over the course of my career, I made many mistakes, but not being able to ask for help was one of the worst. Everyone needs help and guidance. It doesn't mean you are weak or not intelligent; it means you are self-aware and honest.

I worked myself into knots of stress and depression. Many of us do. Asking for help on a project or asking for help with depression and anxiety is a strength. I never looked at it that way. When I was actively playing, I tried to do it on my own. I had always leaned on my dad, but when I became a professional, I didn't want to anymore. I either didn't know what to ask or felt shame in asking for help. I've learned to be more open with my thoughts and emotions. It's a process and not always easy, but I do make an effort.

When I had my elbow surgery, I became so depressed that I didn't care about my life anymore. I wanted to escape my reality and make myself feel better any way I could. It was, by far, the worst time in my life. I was alone. In looking back at some of the most difficult moments in my life, I can see that at the time I was only convincing myself that I was fine. Now, on the other side of the problems, I can see that I was hiding from reality, not facing my problems, and lying to myself constantly. I was not "fine" and couldn't understand that was not okay. Lying to myself only permitted me to continue to look for escapes and stopgap measures to feel stable. It ultimately led to substance abuse and depression. My refusal to accept life's ups and downs and ask for help caused my addiction.

John Patterson 2.0

My substance abuse escalated, and the substances changed. Whatever would allow me to escape from reality is what I did. I was at the point that it didn't really even matter what it was, and gradually my use increased over two years, from the age of twenty-two to twenty-four. When I got home from Arizona in the fall of 2003, I had lost about twenty-five pounds. I was 6'6", 185 pounds, with huge dark circles under my eyes. I was exhausted and self-medicating by taking pills to keep my body feeling level.

I was engaged, and she was doing the exact same thing I was. We were locked in a cyclic downward spiral. One night, we got into a huge fight and, as you can imagine, we were completely off base and toxic to one another. This fight changed my life for the better. I thought, "I'm not doing this anymore; I can't take it. I want to have my career again; I want to take care of me." I broke our engagement, asked for the ring back, and she left.

It was about 2:00 in the morning, and I called my dad, which was a big deal. I had been so against reaching out, but I was now at a tipping point. I told him, "I'm done. I need you to come get me." Ten minutes later, he pulled up in my driveway, and I was outside. I had the garage door open, and I had been pacing in circles around the driveway. When he got there, I just put my arms around him and hugged him. I started crying, went inside, and gave him a little box that had all these drugs in it. Then I said probably one of the most important things in my life, "I don't want to do this anymore. I want to be your son again."

I got in his truck, and he brought me back to my parents' house. I sat there and talked to my mom and dad about how bad the situation had gotten. They cried, I cried, and we put it all out on the table. They helped me start my recovery in a real way.

I had always felt that I had to be so strong and so independent to be successful. Now I know that it doesn't necessarily happen on your own. I thought asking for help was showing some glaring weakness that I wasn't supposed to show. For me to say to one of my coaches, or my dad, just as a person, "Hey, I'm struggling. I need help. I need to see you. I need you to come talk me through this" was just something that I never felt like I could do. If I did that, it had to mean that I wasn't capable in some way, that I couldn't do my job. It felt like a major failing.

When the bottom fell out from underneath me and I had such a major disappointment and sense of failure, I needed to be honest and humble. I felt my dream was now out of my reach, and the despair was multiplied by one hundred when you included my sense of loneliness and patterns of self-destruction.

What changed? From the moment of repairing the relationship I had with my mom and dad, with my family, my brother, and my sister included, I was feeling like I could do it again. Live again. I'd hit rock bottom and there was nowhere else to go but back up. John Patterson 3.0 was being born.

I knew that I needed to be traded. I could not stay in Arizona and complete the process of growing and healing and being able to put my career back online. I had pitched well enough the year before that I knew I could be traded and go play for another big league team. I just didn't know where and you don't really have control of that. So I was back in Arizona in 2004, with all those negative memories and the emotional scar tissue. I wasn't comfortable with management and certain members of the team. I wasn't comfortable with myself yet either, so it wasn't a good environment. I got called into the office the last week of spring training and was told by the general manager I had been traded to Montreal. I was flooded with emotions, and I couldn't wait to call my dad and tell him I was going to get a chance to start over.

The trade to Montreal was huge, and I felt like a completely new person. It was a blank slate, and I could start over. My environment changed, my friends changed, all the things that you hear of to get clean and sober. You change your environment, change your friends. Lots of things have to change. But that was it for me; it was exactly what I needed. I was even in a different country, which felt great, and I could focus on me. I could focus on pitching and get away from thinking the way that I thought before. I was older, wiser, and I'd learned from my mistakes in the past.

I still beat myself up about some of the choices that I made because what I did to myself was pretty awful. It was nothing for my mom to be proud of. I also have to acknowledge though that I would have never met my wife or be living the amazing life that I am now if I had not made those decisions. Based on that alone, I wouldn't change any of it. My relationship with my dad is as strong as it has been since I was a kid.

My relationship with my mom has never wavered, and I feel very close to her. I wholeheartedly accept my blessings along with my mistakes.

Eventually you've got to look at your life experiences as a learning process. You are not defined by your job, your car, your wealth, or your looks any more than I'm defined by a game called baseball. You aren't even defined by your dreams. It has taken me decades to say that, but it is the truth. You just are who you were created to be, and your story—good and bad—will change lives. What if what you went through was for a larger purpose, so that it could help your kids or your grandkids when they hear your story? What if your story changes or even saves someone else's life?

One of my biggest regrets was my response to the surgery I had in 2000. That next year, the Diamondbacks won the World Series. If I would have asked for help, if I would have not abused myself, if I had not felt sorry for myself and drugged myself and beat myself up, and if I had rehabbed faster, then I believe I would have been on that World Series team. It's really hard for me not to say that at some point during that year, probably the second half of the season, I actually could have played on a World Series team. That was a missed opportunity, and that one's kind of hard to swallow. But ultimately it did not happen, and I need to forgive myself. Beating myself up and saying "if only I had done this instead" won't change anything.

The biggest regrets are usually the choices we look back on and realize were the wrong ones, especially when we look at the things that could have been accomplished in the time that was lost while we made self-destructive decisions. It's hard to think on those missed opportunities.

Sometimes you have to seek professional help. You need to be able to talk through things. If you can't get professional help, find someone that you can trust. You need a sounding board who tells you not only what you want to hear, but someone who tells you what you need to hear. I don't think most people's first response is to seek help because sometimes they don't even understand how they're hurting right at the initial moment. There is a stigma applied to people in society, who seek professional help. I've heard people say, "Oh, I could never see a therapist. I'm not crazy." That's completely wrong. Do not listen to those types of people. Therapy helps you discover feelings you didn't even know were there. It helps you see the big picture and analyze why you are acting the way you are. Suppressed feelings and emotions are extremely dangerous to your mental health.

I think of my nephew and a challenge he's facing at the moment. He was tops in his class and was accepted to West Point. He was doing fantastically and made it through his first semester there. This year, he had a problem with his immune system and got sick. He couldn't do the physical work. He could only do the schoolwork, and they sent him home, with the caveat that he could come back once he could do the physical work again. This is the Army, this is West Point, and he could only do half the work. He went from being at one of the most premier colleges in the country to back at home in Orange, Texas, for doctors to diagnose his situation while all his friends carry on their lives at West Point.

He's really struggling right now with being honest about the situation. I can see it because I know him and I've been through a painful situation like this. He just can't be honest about it yet. He's going to hurt until he can take an objective look at the circumstances and decide if what he needs is a new path or if he'll be able to get back to West Point. And so, all he's doing is getting more and more depressed and he's sleeping more. We're all really worried about him, but he hasn't been able to ask for help yet. He says, "I'm okay, I'm okay; it's going to be all right." If we could only see into the future and know that this puts him on the path for his next big success. But, being in this moment, it is hard to see any positives.

I think the first step for anyone is acknowledging that you were not okay and that your dream has changed, your life just changed, and the path has changed. There was a fork in the road, and you were forced down a different path that you didn't see coming, and that's okay. Plans change. Dreams change.

We all dislike change and feeling vulnerable. We just don't know how to say in words that we're not okay. Why is it humans can't reach out to others when we are in need? We present our best selves to the world. It's as if our agent is responding instead. We shy away from showing our most vulnerable self, yet everyone has the same issues, obstacles, fears, and sufferings. There are moments of victory in life and times of questioning, or setback.

I saw the funniest meme recently that said, "Don't forget to pretend to have your life together for strangers on the internet today."

When we hit bottom, most people never want anyone to see. And, it's not like you only hit the bottom once. You're going to hit the bottom plenty of times. When it happens to you, take it as an opportunity to shift your perceptions. Think, how do I want to change the way that I see the bottom? How do

I change my own behavior when others are going through a rough time? What can I learn from this?

A speaker once said that rock bottom is the best foundation to begin building from! You need to build on solid ground, and what could be more solid than that? Rock bottom is not the end. It is the new beginning.

It's not where everything stops. Instead it's like a swimming pool. When you let yourself sink to the bottom, it's the point where you bend your knees, you brace yourself, you push off, and you get back to the top. It's just the way that we bounce back. Everybody's going to hit the bottom at some point, but don't stay under the water and drown. Brace yourself and push back to the surface.

You have a choice at the bottom to push up or stay there, and it's a decision that we make for ourselves. What happens when it's time to reach out for help because we just can't do it ourselves? Reach out. Whether it's a stranger or a friend or a pastor or a family member—don't risk not getting help. We've all been there. Even the very best leader has hit rock bottom and learned from it.

It's okay to not be okay.

We can be ruled by fear, or we can speak out. "I'm not okay today, but I'll probably be okay tomorrow. I'm not okay today, and it's okay to admit that I'm not okay today." Sometimes, it's even okay to say, "I think I'll stay home and eat ice cream and watch Netflix, but tomorrow I'm going to push off the bottom." It's okay to feel those emotions. It's a valid place to be; just don't pack up and move to the bottom of the pool.

It is a choice. If you do stay down there, you chose to stay down there. It is the worst and most selfish choice you can make, and only you are responsible for it, you make it. When I struggle in my life now, the thought of my son and my family always gives me hope. Sometimes you have to be willing to set aside your own emotions for the feelings of others, and reach out for that light in the darkness. Movement, going to an activity or taking a walk—all of these things are a step in the right direction.

Depression and anxiety can be part of your journey and sometimes they can pop up when things look like they're going perfectly. I can remember a day back in 2003. I was miserable. I was in the big leagues, but I wasn't happy or excited about being there. We were on the field getting ready to stretch, and Curt Schilling said to me, "You do realize there is no five A, right?" His point was there is no level higher than where I was. It was the pinnacle of baseball, and I was depressed and had major anxiety. The year had not gone how I had hoped, and my substance abuse had increased. From the outside looking in, I'm sure there were thousands of players who would have loved to be standing where I was standing, but I was dying on the inside. This is a good example of why you shouldn't compare your life to someone else's life. You have no idea what they are battling internally.

Recently I had extreme suicidal thoughts, and it was a really rough day for me. I felt like the world was coming down on top of me. I felt like a failure, I felt like people hated me, and every negative thought you could possibly be thinking hit me all at one time. All I kept focusing on was what if I wasn't here. If I committed suicide, if I died, my son wouldn't have a father. I would be leaving my family with anguish and sadness, and I didn't want to do that.

Saying it out loud, just verbalizing it. There's power to even saying it out loud to yourself, because we hide those thoughts deep inside our heads. It helps me to be able to trust myself to say it and to trust somebody to hear it. When you say it out loud, you can hear that little voice in your head that has been drowned out by negativity say, "That's a little extreme. Right?" It forces you to take a step back.

You have to shift your focus when these negative thoughts come up. I focused more on my family and not myself, until I could get a grip on my situation. What makes a person go from being successful, clean, and sober to being in a hospital, suffering from an overdose? Over the last few years, many celebrities have committed suicide, and we can't figure out why someone who "has it all" would kill themselves. Something was triggered in a flash, and life just didn't feel worth it anymore.

Those dark moments can make you lose sight of what is really important, the people that love you the most, and you can start feeling like you are alone and that nothing matters. When I have felt like I don't matter and nothing matters, I'll just go destroy myself in some way, it's because I'm thinking selfishly and I'm thinking only about myself. I could say that with 100 percent certainty, in every single instance.

When you are sitting at the bottom of the pool, you have to remember what helped you float or jolt back up each time. For me, it is my wife. She comforts me. She calms me down and, in a lot of ways, makes me feel like everything is going to be okay. You have to find somebody that you can talk to whether that is walking into a church or calling a hotline, a best friend, or a family member. It has to be somebody that you can call and actually say the words and just release it. If you can release it, many times it will break the cycle and help you snap out of it. When you verbalize it, it makes it more real and brings more

attention to the actual harm you're doing to yourself. To actually say it to yourself is one thing, but to say it to someone in
your personal life, "Hey, I'm suicidal, I'm hurting" takes a different kind of courage. I had to do this recently. I walked into
the room and looked at my wife and said, "I'm not good; this
is what's going on." She listened and as soon as I said it, I could
feel it. Peace. Relief. I started calming down, and we talked.
Being able to verbalize these feelings is probably the most important thing you're going to be able to do for yourself.

I know that I'm not good when I'm alone. When you are
suffering from depression and anxiety, being alone is what
puts you in the dark. And, it keeps you there.

Those self-destructive behaviors can run through us because we have no accountability. The lack of accountability
actually makes me more depressed. I need people around me
to keep me on the path toward the person I want to be.

This is the ongoing conversation my parents and I had about
being drafted straight out of high school at eighteen years
old, having a huge bank account from my signing bonus, and
skipping all of the emotional development and life skills that
you gain in college. I thought with all the money in my bank
account and being drafted number five that I knew what I was
doing. It felt like the minor league coaches resented me for
the amount of money I made at such a young age. I had more
money in my bank account than everyone in that clubhouse
combined, and money changes everything. Money changes it
into a business. That resentment from the coaches and other
players made the pitcher's mound feel like a deserted island
that I was on alone. No one helped me stay accountable to my
goals or truly coached me. I would go out and pitch, and get
no feedback, so I would go out and make the same mistakes

again. I was lost and didn't have anyone to help me pick up the pieces. With already being a perfectionist and then being thrown into this environment, it was a time bomb waiting to go off. I wanted to be perfect, and the coaches expected it.

There was an expectation for perfection that I felt that I needed to show to validate the amount of money I signed for. What I didn't get was how I felt as though many people wanted to see me fail, including some of the coaches.

My idea of pro ball was that everyone would be going in the same direction. Coaches would be awesome, and we would get on the bus, win games, and get along. I thought I was going to finally feel like part of a team. With no coaching and no accountability, I was isolated and began to rebel in the box I felt forced into. I was an exceptional talent, who needed guidance and a role model. I didn't have either and spiraled out of control.

Present day, I have gone back to my accountability partners, namely my parents, Shannon, and Palmer, my son. Shannon has always been honest with me. She is the person who could step in and say, "Hey, you're drinking too much." It would probably start a fight, but I always knew she was right because I trust her opinion.

Depression

Shannon's pretty good about being able to get me to get up and go and do things and be around people. Once I'm there, I'm fine. It's the initial get up and go part that I think a lot of people struggle with. It's the anxiety that I built up in my head about what people would ask me. I wasn't comfortable with where I was in my life, and I thought they would look at me like a failure. It took me a long time to realize that people just wanted to talk to me about the positives of baseball or other things I was passionate about. They wanted to hear about pitching in front of fifty-five thousand fans or playing with Randy Johnson. All I could think about were the negatives or failures of my career. I was projecting my negative thoughts on them. Guess what? When you project negative thoughts, you get negative reactions back. Imagine how the page would turn if you started projecting positivity.

There is hope. There is always hope.

When I was twenty-three years old, I didn't expect to live to forty. I don't know exactly why, but I was okay with that and I never told anyone. At twenty-three, I thought I was going to go as hard as I possibly could, I'd be dead by forty, and that would be it. That would be fine. Right? The only thing I wanted to do was play baseball and be my definition of successful. As soon as that success was over, fine. I wouldn't have anybody to explain it to, and I'll just be gone.

If I had not asked for help, I would have lost my career at twenty-four and probably would have died much sooner than forty. Instead, I got my relationship back with my family, and two years later, I had the best year of my career in the Major Leagues. It was amazing. I finished in the top 10 of the National League in ERA and strikeouts and was nominated for Top Performance of the Year. In September of that year, I met Shannon, and two years later, we were married. Life had different plans for me. And it can have numerous alternative plans for you too. Be vocal and take back the power you gave to your negative thoughts.

Chapter 5

DON'T BE ENTITLED

In sports, you often hear the phrase, "Nothing is given, and everything is earned."

In sports, business, or life, success can sometimes lead to feelings of entitlement. It's not just athletes who end up feeling entitled without realizing it. It can be leaders, too. Entitlement is when someone acts as if they deserve something more than others. Maybe they were once poor and then achieved wealth and ended up acting as if they deserved the best things in life or deserved more than anyone else. This happens a lot when people lose perspective of the rest of the world or where they came from. It also can occur when people forget to be grateful, so recognize that just because you're on top today, doesn't mean you will be tomorrow. There's always someone who wants what you have.

If you are feeling good about yourself, you are putting off this energy or attitude that you know it all. There is a fine line between being confident and being arrogant. I had an extreme amount of confidence in my talent, but I did not have an extreme amount of confidence in other people. My dad taught me to listen to coaches and I would. But if I went out and didn't have immediate success from what they taught me, I would write those coaches off and not listen to them anymore. I am a fighter because of my experiences in high school. I had baseball coaches who were really football coaches. They coached with aggression, and it taught me how to tune people out and build a wall around myself. I wasn't going to let other people tell me who I was or what I was going to do.

Working hard and doing your best doesn't always mean that you will get what you want, or even what you think you deserve. When I was in high school, I thought I'll do my schoolwork, train after school, be a good teammate, and I'd get a college scholarship. This isn't true. The same can be said in the course of any career. Life just happens.

We aren't guaranteed anything. Some people think if I do my job and I work hard, it may enter my mind that I deserve a promotion. This isn't true either. Expect to give your best without receiving anything in return. You are being paid to do your job. You shouldn't expect to receive more just for doing your job.

I had a strong sense of entitlement when I was in High Single A and Double A. If I strung together a few great starts, I wanted to be promoted immediately to the next level. Instead, they would keep me where I was facing the same batters and being on the same bus to the same small towns over and over again. What I didn't understand at the time was that there were people in front of me, and they wanted me to get consistent experiences. They would tell me the big league coaches were watching me, and I would get moved up soon, but it wouldn't happen. It started building up my entitlement and resentment at the same time.

As kids, we are taught that hard work leads to success. Somewhere along the line it seems as if the message has been changed, and that success now seems to be expected automatically without the hard work. That is entitlement. In a world where everyone is comparing their progress on social media, it can be easy to fall into the trap of believing the path will be easy.

I wasn't immune to it, and when I was nineteen years old in my first year in professional baseball, I wasn't aware of my own sense of entitlement. I was overconfident. I didn't know how hard the next steps would be. I thought, "This is going to be fun." In some ways it was fun, but it was a pressure cooker. There was pressure from all directions, all the time. It never occurred to me that it would be a constant process of earning respect and creating solid results. What I wish I knew then is there's no finish line; the work and effort never stops.

My first spring training was in Yuma, Arizona. My first game was against the San Diego Padres Double A Team. I had only thrown bullpens and batting practice to live hitters at that point. I had had success and was getting patted on the back by coaches and players. It was fun times and boosted my ego. Going into the game against the Padres, I was confident, but nervous. I knew I was going to be facing good hitters. It was a beautiful night, and the stands were full. You could tell when I was warming up everyone was excited to see me throw my first game. I remember standing in center field and throwing my long toss to the third base line and feeling great. Then, I stepped on to the mound and started facing batters. I struck a few out, but then the batters started hitting my best pitches. They were hitting my fastballs that I used to be able to blow right past the batters. If I struck them out the first time, the next time they got up to bat, they were ready for me. These guys were good! After the game, I had a small panic attack and was somewhat depressed because it didn't go exactly how I wanted it to go. I went back to my hotel room and sat down at the desk and started writing. I wrote down all of my thoughts of what I needed to do better. My roommate, Ben Norris, just sat there and laughed at me. He had played in short season after the draft the year before I had missed from signing later. He had already experienced what it was like to play professionally coming out of high school. Ben told me that it doesn't mean that you are not good; it means that they are really good too. We can become entitled thinking we are the best. You might be, but there are also a lot of other incredibly talented people out there.

When I coach and work with kids now, there's always this sense of some grand finish line. There is the expectation that when you reach a certain point, and the work is done. The truth is that you finished the day. You either had a successful day or you didn't, but tomorrow's another day and so is the day after that. You have to continue to learn pitching mechanics or mental thought processes for the game. There is no single answer of achievement to unlock. There are just answers for today and then you build on it the next day and the next day, and the next day. Being trapped in an entitled mind-set means you miss the lesson that, yes you've succeeded, but you haven't yet embraced the idea of constant personal growth and evolution.

To truly be successful, you have to earn it; the world owes you nothing. You can only control the processes of learning and growing.

There are many different modes of entitlement in people's minds. In my case, my sense of entitlement stemmed from the thought that since I had been successful in the past, I would continue to be successful. If you are modeling your perceived entitlement to success because of past successes, you are setting yourself up for crushing and debilitating feelings of failure in the future.

In 2005, the Montreal Expos team moved to Washington, DC. Going into the Spring Training, I did not have a spot in the starting rotation. I knew going in that I needed to be at the top of my game to make the team. We had a new general manager named Jim Bowden. He watched everything I did and was constantly pushing me and giving me confidence. After everything I had been through, he was giving me exactly what I needed to succeed. I wasn't entitled anymore. I focused on what I could control, kept my head down, and worked.

I was throwing the ball really well and was physically very strong. It was looking like I was going to be the long relief pitcher out of the bullpen, but that's not what I wanted. I wanted to be a starter. Toward the end of Spring Training, one of the starters pulled a hamstring, and it opened up the opportunity for me in the rotation. I never looked back and never came out of the rotation again. That season was everything I and so many people had always believed I was capable of. If I had been entitled and expected the spot in the rotation, I know I would not have won the spot. I had a chip on my shoulder and was determined to win the spot, not be given the spot.

Many times, we often inadvertently compare ourselves to others. If I did the same job as my coworker and they received a raise, surely I deserve one too. It's too easy to shift your focus on achievements and what others are doing to the point of losing sight of your own tasks and responsibilities. When our expectations aren't being met, there's an almost natural inclination to give less because we feel our efforts aren't being rewarded. This is self-limiting thinking, and you are capping your own potential. Maybe you didn't get that raise, but you surely won't get the next one because you aren't doing your best work.

Instead, focus on you, your task, and your way to win the day. Then get up the next day and start over and do it again. Whether you have success or failure or just a blur of a day, try to improve the next day. There has to be a day-to-day process of being organized, having a task, attacking the task, doing the best that you can do, and understanding that you're going to crawl a lot of the time. But that's the challenge. Tomorrows are always different than the day before.

In 2005, I had fourteen no decisions and got a loss in seven games when I gave up one or no runs in seven innings or more pitched. I was not getting any run support. It was so frustrating, but I knew that if I pouted and became careless, I would hurt my team and ruin my season. After pitching a great game one night, a reporter asked me, "What is your breaking point because of your lack of run support?" I looked in his face and laughed. "What good would that do?" Am I supposed to quit? I'm not guaranteed a win because I pitched well. You aren't guaranteed a promotion or a raise because you did your job.

In August that year, I faced the Los Angeles Dodgers. This game was against Brad Penny, my longtime nemesis. We had played our first three years together for the Arizona Diamondbacks and Team USA. Brad was not a first-round draft pick but was an extremely talented pitcher. He was big, strong, and extremely competitive. He was always competing against me, and we had more than one run-in when we played together for the Diamondbacks. He had always thought I was the top dog and he was the underdog. It was the first time the roles had been reversed on me. He was using me as motivation the same way I had used top pitchers when I was the underdog. Normally it is a guy on the other team and not the same team. We had a lot of battles against each other on and off the field. After we finished with Team USA, he was traded to the Florida Marlins, and I went to Triple A. The next spring training was when I had my elbow surgery. At the same time I had this going on, he got called up to the big leagues and was cruising along. This was something that added to my depression after being hurt because I watched the success of his career while I was sitting on a couch in a brace.

That night in 2005 was the first time we had ever faced each other in the big leagues. Both of our teams knew our history of battling each other. All my teammates were pumped and ready to help me battle. The first inning, I struck out a couple of guys. The next inning, I struck out a few more. I came up to bat the second inning, and Penny threw a ball up and in. I jumped back and glared at him. He came off the mound yelling at me. I went back to the dugout and told my team that the next at bat he has it coming, I am going to hit him.

The coaches came over and talked me out of it. They were telling me I had a good game going and not to ruin it. The next inning, I struck out all three batters, three up and three down. At this point, I had racked up quite a few strikeouts. I don't remember how many at that point, but everyone was into it: the umpires, the crowd, my team, and of course me. I don't think I had even given up a hit at that point. The bleachers at RFK Stadium were on wheels, so they could change the stadium from baseball to football. When the crowd jumped, the entire stands would bounce and rattle. The louder they got and the more they jumped, the more I pushed.

The moment became surreal. It was a noise and feeling that I can still feel today when I close my eyes. My strikeouts kept rolling in: ten, eleven, and twelve. The ball was jumping out of my hand. It was baseball at its finest. We ended up winning the game, and I had thirteen strikeouts, but the biggest thing to me was beating my all-time nemesis. It was my breakout time. It was emotionally validating to me on a deeply personal level. It was the culmination of the years of pain. That game means more to me than all of them combined.

I ended that season competing against one of my all-time Texas heroes, Roger Clemens,, for the National League ERA title. He had a 2.20 ERA and I had a 2.40 ERA going into my last three starts of the season. Competing against Roger blew my mind. This was an enormous deal to me. I didn't finish the season the way I wanted to, but I still landed in the top 10 for ERA. But that's not the point. It was the culmination of years of injuries, pain, and depression. I was finally healthy and living up to my potential.

I've been humbled a lot in the course of my life, and I've also had a lot of success. My goal now is to try to find balance, where I can put things into true perspective and guide my thoughts to knowing that I'm doing something and getting better as a person. Perfection has always been my biggest demon. I have always been a perfectionist. I always wanted the best. I always expected the best from my peers. At the end of the day, putting forth an effort and trying every day is actually "the best."

Have you ever considered that entitlement may be coloring your definition of success?

My wife and I spoke recently about success in terms of feelings of entitlement. Success for one person might be a million dollars, but for someone else maybe it's ten million dollars. For another person it could be as simple and beautiful as a happy family. There are so many variables in success that you have to have the right perspective. This is another reason why you should never compare yourself to other people. You don't know anything about another person's success or what is hiding behind the curtain. If your perspective of success is being a team leader at work and owning a Ferrari, but you're not quite there yet, does that make you a failure? No!

Do you disregard the hard work you put in or remain dissatisfied with driving a nice SUV? Of course not. Entitlement says, "That Ferrari should be mine," but humility answers, "I worked hard for that SUV, and someday I will get that Ferrari."

We were all created to be very different so that we could rely on each other's talents for success in family life, business, athletics, or the corner office.

My wife is a former beauty queen and had a tremendous amount of success in her pageant life. She was fourth runner-up to Miss America in 2006 and was top six at Mrs. America in 2010. She's currently a board member of the Miss District of Columbia Organization and trains the winners for Miss America. Recently we had a Miss DC in town. She was getting ready for Miss America in a few weeks, and I was working with her on her interview. In my twelve years or so of being around pageants, I have yet to meet a state winner who didn't think they were going to win Miss America. We ask them, "Why should you be Miss America?" I would say more than seven out of ten answer they want it more than everyone else. They can see themselves with that crown on their head just because they want it. This is an entitlement that we all have to a certain extent. We believe we deserve it.

In my youth, my identity was so strongly defined by my perception as a baseball player. I thought it was the most "valuable" part of who I was. Of course it is natural if you have an athletic ability or talent to focus on it. But then as time went by, it became my only worth.

This came from insecurity and projecting my self-worth into what I thought would be best for others' perception of me. There really was no plan other than my baseball career. My confidence, self-worth, and value in only baseball served in defining my view of success. But what if we could teach our youth differently?

As a youth, I never asked myself the hard questions. Who am I? What if my career ended?

There was no other option and no plan B. This was a type of entitlement and maybe a bit of a false expectation. I couldn't see a future without professional baseball. Even if I played baseball until I was forty, I still have another thirty-five to forty years of life left. Baseball was always going to end, whether I was twenty-nine or forty.

If I wanted it, surely it would happen. But then I faced a hard reality. If you only define yourself as that one thing and then that thing is gone, what do you live for? You don't know who you are, and because you found your worth in what is gone, you're not complete in any sense of the word now. You put yourself into a box and that's it. It's over. You have to find your truth, the definition of yourself, so that when the job you do falls through, you are still you. You can still move forward, knowing that another job or another opportunity is waiting around the corner.

What do you care about? I was a good student up until my sophomore year in high school, then I no longer cared about school. The only reason I went to school was because of baseball. I had such good, loving parents who wanted me to accomplish my dreams, that they started doing my schoolwork for me. My mom would do my homework. My sister and my girlfriend would do school projects, and all I did was train. I would lift weights, go to the track, run, and meet my dad at the baseball field. We would practice until it got dark and the Texas mosquitos had eaten us alive. I would get home mentally drained and physically exhausted. I didn't have the energy to sit there and read a book or do homework that I cared nothing about. I didn't need it. I was going to be a big leaguer. A better answer would have been I want to a big leaguer and then I want to be an entrepreneur and author. It's a more complete idea of what life is about. We should not define ourselves by one idea of who we are or by what we do.

Because there was only that one focus on my mind from such a young age, it really did become who I was. It was the beginning of losing myself to what I wanted. I can say now, that's not the right way to do it. My parents and I realized later, though very well intentioned, their help became a handicap. I didn't cook. I didn't clean. I didn't do things that normal kids have to do to continue to grow and mature. Instead, I became entitled and expected that I could just focus on what was important to me and someone else would do the rest. It was all great until I was twenty-nine and my elbow gave out. I didn't have anything else; I didn't know anything else.

To be a complete person, you have to think of yourself beyond what you've trained for and about who you are beyond your self-imposed labels. You will only get so far if you're not a complete person. If you have early success and you have a career that you've defined as what you want, it's not who you are. It's how you use that success that defines you as a person.

Baseball players used to joke about this all the time. "The career is so short, you're on borrowed time." Most people have business careers where they'll work until they retire. What do they do after that? What are their passions? Have they even taken the time in their forty years of working to figure that out?

As an athlete, you're built to be invincible and be strong. You don't ever think about the fact you're only holding your spot for right now. Entitlement. At some point, your team, organization, or company is not going to want you anymore. Or, maybe you aren't going to be able to do the job anymore. You're just sitting on borrowed time.

Your legacy is what you leave behind. I had always thought my legacy would be as a ballplayer, but with my time in professional baseball, I now understand that isn't true, and it is only a small part.

Who are you? And if you think you know, are you continuing to work for it?

How do you use your success to help improve who you are? Charity? Mentorship?

Who are you outside of your career life? What are you doing to understand better who you are?

Make a commitment to yourself to find out who you are beyond what you do.

Chapter 6

CONTROL

I believed I was in control of my life's outcomes. I believed control was based on work ethic and focus. When I realized that was not a fact, I would lose focus on the important things and focus on things I couldn't control. I wanted to dictate my day, week, and future on my terms. Having change or lack of control would totally disrupt my goals. I would let small things ruin my day or force me to make changes I didn't want to make. Being rigid in needing to be in control of outcomes forced me into depression and feelings of failure.

What do you do when you lose control or when the bad days and unforeseen events knock you off a positive run toward your goals? Remember that you can never be fully prepared for all of the variables. Sometimes it is completely out of our hands. Perceiving failure or thinking we can always be in complete control is a blind spot. During The Conversation Event in Dallas that Tammy Kling and her team put together every year in the fall, I had the opportunity to be in a circle surrounded by incredibly successful world changers from all over the world. It helped me realize that control was my blind spot. This is a blind spot for a lot of people. It is easy to deceive ourselves into believing that because we have gained some life experience or we have a good work ethic, we control our lives. The real growth happens when we realize that control is an illusion. Think about your life. You don't control the outcomes, and you don't control what happens next. You can have everything completely and exactly where you want it, but you could be driving down the highway and another car can alter your entire future. You don't have any control over that. You only have control over how you respond.

As an athlete, I felt I was invincible. I truly believed that no matter what, I was going to be a successful Major League player with a long and successful career. When I was young, I had no reason *not* to believe that outcome. It wasn't until I injured my elbow for the third time and was forced to retire in the prime of my career, that I realized I had no control over my outcomes. That is the variable that never crosses your mind. Life can change in an instant. One pitch and it was over. How do we live knowing that we don't control the outcome? We focus on the variables that we can control.

At the age of twenty-seven, I was at the top of my game. I was coming off the best year of my career, and I had also met my future wife. It was spring training 2006, we had a beautiful condo on the beach in Cape Canaveral, Florida, and I was feeling great. I had matured and was as healthy as I had ever been. I had the best spring I had ever had statistically and physically, but during my last start of the spring, I felt a pop in my elbow. The next morning, I looked down at my arm. It was swollen, and something was different. I could hardly move it up and down.

I had done everything right to get myself back on track: I had gotten myself back under control, I wasn't drinking, and I wasn't smoking. I wasn't doing anything. I had removed every negative thing that could hold me back. How could this happen? Well, I don't know. I spent years dwelling on that question. That moment ultimately ended my career. There were two more elbow surgeries, and I never pitched again. There are a thousand things I could blame. Ultimately, I had to come to the realization that I didn't control that. I did what I could do. Sometimes you don't do anything to cause something bad to happen. I just threw the pitch, I did my job, I did what I was supposed to be doing, and my life changed immediately, not once, but three times in my career.

The freedom came when I let it go. I don't control what happens when I get in my car and pull out of my driveway. I can control staying in my lane, but that motorcycle all of a sudden comes out of nowhere. I have no control over that, right? That's life. Now I remind myself, my wife, and my son daily that you can only control what you can control. You make the choice of how you respond.

What do we control? We control our attitude, our response, our work ethic, and our faith. Your life is more than your dreams because God has a better plan for you. He has control, not you. I believed because I had worked so hard and spent so many hours focusing on my goals, that I was in control. God gave me all of my talents I know about, and He also knows all the talents I have not yet discovered.

I was a selfish and narrow-thinking young adult, but now I see more of a big picture for my life. My wife has always told me that something even greater is coming for me. I am finally able to see that happening. I see the ability to help many more people with my story and experiences than with playing baseball. This is a healthy response, but it's not the first one I chose. I had to go through all the responses of grieving the loss of my career to get to where I am now. There are two types of people in life: the ones who learn from other people's mistakes and the ones who learn from their own mistakes. I always wanted to learn on my own terms.

I grew up in the First Baptist Church of Orange, Texas. My mom sang in the choir, and my parents taught Sunday School. I grew up knowing God and was baptized around the age of ten. I could feel God working in my life, but I didn't feel I could give all of my life to Him. I held back control. I wanted to have some say in my direction in life. If I gave God complete control, maybe I would get an answer to prayer that I didn't like or want. It can be scary to trust so deeply that you have no control over your preferred outcomes. Have you ever heard the saying, "If it's meant to be, it will be?" I'm sure I had said it many times in my adolescence, but I didn't believe it. I believed that if you worked hard enough and put yourself in the right positions, you would have success and control your desired outcome. I learned a very hard lesson that life isn't about what I want, it's about what God has planned for me. In fighting my arrogance of perceived control, I became an extremely unhappy and depressed person. It made me an addict, and I pushed God further away. Please don't take this path. Believe in something bigger than yourself and have faith.

When we lose the perspective that life is going to go on beyond a moment of change, we can make bad choices. Have you hit bottom when you were running straight for your dreams? It isn't over! It's changed and it's going to be better.

My faith was weak. My attitude became poor, and my response was negative. My failure was the reaction, not the action. If I would have spent time on my knees praying and asking God for answers, I would have had a positive attitude and a more productive response. My faith would have grown, my light would have shined brightly, and I could have been a role model for another young teammate. Instead, I was negative, dark, and a poor role model. I focused on what I didn't have and what I couldn't control. I learned the lesson, but it took many years of pain.

The choices that you have are yours. You can either move forward, or you can crumble and fall into the destructive path that can lead to addiction, bankruptcy, homelessness, divorce, or even suicide. The biggest truth is that you control the choice of overcoming or succumbing to the changes of life. You know that the answer is not in giving up. You may not be able to control what happened, but you can control how you respond.

You won't always make the right choice. Bouncing back is a skill. Things in your life are going to go up and down. The stock market in the nineties was shooting straight up through the technology boom. No one saw it coming when the recession hit. Just like when life hits us hard and drops us to our knees, we have to recalibrate. If you look at the stock market now, it dropped off but has been steadily climbing with dips here and there. But it still continues that upward path.

Ten years from now, you are going to look over the course of your life, and you are going to see that upward path. Yes, there will have been dips, but if you stay consistent, stay in the right frame of mind, and know that it's not always going to go straight up and that there will be bumps in the road, you will be prepared, no matter what comes your way. Why? Because you were prepared for the bumps in the road. Acknowledging they're going to be there means they're no surprise. It's easier to stay positive knowing that when things are going really, really well, at some point it's going to change, and when it does change, you can shrug it off and think, "Yes, that's life, and I know how to respond."

My wife bought me a cross with the Serenity Prayer on it. It sits next to my bathroom sink. Every morning, I read it and reflect on its meaning for my day.

Serenity Prayer

God, grant me the serenity to accept the things I cannot change,

The courage to change the things I can,

And the wisdom to know the difference.

THINGS TO THINK ON:

- How do you handle loss of control? Do you see it as an opportunity for growth, or do you feel defeated?

- What is the positive in the negative?

- Will you vow to give up control in order to live your purpose?

- How could you change your life if you focused on being positive first?

Chapter 7

FACING ADVERSITY

Adversity and failure work together. We all face adversity in our lives. Many times, we have to face it in our personal and career lives at the same time. The toughest adversity I have ever had to face was after my second and third elbow surgeries. I had gone through so many hardships, some self-inflicted and some not, to get myself on the path to a happier and healthier life, both professionally and personally, and in an instant, it all was over. I went from the best year of my life at twenty-six years old to having back-to-back elbow surgeries at twenty-seven and twenty-eight and being out of the game at twenty-nine. Trying to understand and gain some perspective on "What does all of this mean?" was mind-boggling.

Adversity comes at you like a ninja. You never see it coming. What do I do now? I'm twenty-nine years old, newly married, and just got released because I physically couldn't throw a baseball anymore. I was angry, sad, confused, lost, tired, and in a strange way relieved. I had basically spent the last two years traveling North America, trying to find a doctor who could tell me what was wrong with my arm and fix it so that I could get back to doing the only thing I knew how to do: pitch. It was a new low.

The adversity was no longer in pitching and learning how to play baseball at the highest level. It was what do I do with the rest of my life? The only skill I had was throwing a baseball. It was extremely scary, and I really had no answer for myself. How would I make money? What should I do with my time? Who am I without baseball?

Depression started to overwhelm me, and I started to drink more and more. My wife and parents were very supportive and told me to take time to heal. There was no rush to make any decisions. I would drink and then back off and repeat what I was doing. Round and round I would go. I made a few investments that didn't work out over the next few years and that made me feel hopeless. Adversity was kicking my butt. I started to realize I was putting my value and my future in other people's hands. I decided I was going to take it into my own hands and start a new company—my own company, with me in control of my future.

You've taken the hard first step, recognized the honest truth, and said it out loud. But what comes next?

You face adversity head-on.

My perception of myself had always been that I was a baseball player. Nothing more and nothing less. That perception caused me to believe that was all anyone else thought of me as well. I began to realize I could do anything I wanted to do if I would just try. I would need to learn a new skill and make some sacrifices, but I could do anything I wanted.

My wife is a real estate broker, and I had always had an attraction to the profession. After many discussions, I started Orange Tree Capital Investments. It was a proud moment for us. I wanted to build houses and develop property. Everywhere I look I see adversity, but I also see opportunity. Adversity surrounds us, and if we let it, it will consume us with fear. I'm going to make mistakes and I'm going to have some failures, but it will not define me. It will sharpen me, just like it will for you. It will prepare me for the next hurdle, and each time it will be a little easier to handle.

I have overcome addiction, arm surgeries, bad investments, bad decisions, and bad friendships. I have overcome adversity, but it does not mean I will not face more. You will never be in the clear. That ninja is always lurking in the darkness to jump out and surprise you.

At the end of the day, I realized I was fighting my own perceptions and the perceptions I thought others had of me. I couldn't figure out what I was going to do next because I perceived not defining myself as a baseball player was admitting failure. I had not failed. I played at the highest level possible for four years and 126 days. The average Major League career is four years. I guess I'm 126 days better than average. There are 3.4 million youth baseball players, and only 1,200 will play in the Major Leagues. That's .0003 percent. I should celebrate that accomplishment, not dwell on the injuries.

Our perceptions of ourselves can be an adversary. Having a positive perception of yourself is probably the most important gift you can grant yourself. It's your energy. You're going to either give off a negative energy or a positive energy; people are going to respond to you based on that energy. If you dwell on your last project, missed deadline, poor meeting, or negative interaction you've had, those feelings will impact your dealings with everyone else. The seeds of negativity have been planted with thoughts like: I didn't succeed at that, I didn't do a good job, and I didn't show leadership. People can be incredibly aware when something doesn't feel quite right with your energy and when you aren't in your best frame of mind. You are giving off this energy. People aren't randomly thinking negative things about you.

Your inner sense of tranquility and self-acceptance is a powerful tool in your interactions with people. My mentality has gotten so much better. I can be myself and not worry about everything else. Adversity can drag you down into a dark place.

If you've done the work and taken a good look at the reality beyond false perceptions, how do you move forward? How do you push toward positivity and break free of toxic thoughts?

We human beings are our own worst enemies. We impose so many negative behaviors on ourselves to meet unrealistic expectations or goals. Struggling to meet these expectations or goals can lead to things like addiction, depression, anxiety, and self-harming. We live in a society that constantly pushes us to do more, faster, bigger, and better than everyone else. Society seems to glorify being so busy that it's almost a status symbol. It's no wonder we set such unreasonable goals to begin with.

This isn't to say that we shouldn't "dream big" or "reach for the stars," but more that our own personal health and well-being are equally important on that road to our ideal aspirations. You are so much more than just your goals, and you deserve to honor the spirit of who you are as a flawed individual but a work in progress.

Maintaining your positivity is a constant process. What do you do when you're in a good place and feel the inklings of negativity at the edges of your mind?

In my experience, there are three things that really make a difference.

1. Pray.

Maybe you don't pray, but you can try to find the positive in the situation and express gratitude for it. A lot of the time just vocalizing what you're thankful for helps you to realize how much is going right, despite anything you feel isn't exactly the way you'd like it to be.

Find the positive in any situation, and it will give you a different perspective. Yes, it can be hard. The answer you find in prayer might not be the answer that you're looking for, but ultimately, you know it's the right answer, the right thing. Knowing and acknowledging what's right is a step in a positive direction. Then act on it and make a conscious decision to come out of the dark and back into the light. I've worked myself back onto the right path and away from the place that is wrong, dreary, and depressed. Focus on the positives, be thankful, and keep doing better.

Sometimes I'll say a little prayer, nothing too complicated, but small, short, and to the point. I hand things over to God and feel relief in knowing that everything will work out. There's a comfort in knowing that something or someone larger than myself has got my back.

2. Visualization and Breathing

Visualization was always part of my preparation for games. Visualize yourself doing something over and over and over again, so when you're in that situation, you just react because you've done it before. Your brain is prepared, and it's no longer a surprise. When I talked about my memory being blacked-out during my first start, it was because I had visualized that moment for years. When the time came, my body and mind knew what I had to do.

You've seen yourself overcome adversity and have a good perception of yourself. You've seen yourself have a good meeting, have a good game, or throw a certain pitch. Visualize it and replicate it in real life.

Breathing is something that I've learned over the last fifteen years. When I can slow myself down and breathe, I get a completely different feeling and I can see myself coming up with a solution, figuring a way out of where I'm stuck. I'm able to understand now that tomorrow will be a different day. Previously, I would let that one day affect the next seven or eight or nine days. I couldn't let it go. I dwelled on it, but breathing and visualization have helped with that. Before you send that email or snap back at your co-worker, client, or child, try taking a series of deep breaths. It can help break the cycle of fighting fire with fire.

As individuals, we feel we are completely in control of every little thing, and that's very damaging. It's damaging in all parts of our lives because life just doesn't work like that. It's very rare when it does. It's humility that reminds us that no, I'm not in full control of anything. I have to just accept it for what it is, try my best, breathe, and let it go.

3. Meditation

Meditation gives us the opportunity to block out the noises that surround us. Noises are negative thoughts, worries, schedules, failures, and everyday distractions. They are also e-mails, kids, TV, social media, and anything else that keeps you from having peace of mind. Take personal time to center yourself and gain focus on your purpose. When is the last time you took a few minutes of quiet time for yourself? I mean true quiet time to focus on your wellbeing and soul. Are the noises loud even when everything is turned off around you?

Meditation is more than sitting on a mat cross-legged and humming. The most recent time I meditated wasn't easy. I like to sit in silence and allow my mind to relax. On this day, I just couldn't get where I wanted to be. I'm trying to get the wheels to stop for a while, but all of my recent failures just kept pulling on my mind and heart. It can be difficult to relax at first because we are so used to going at a fast pace. It's amazing how many thoughts are going on in our head when we try to force them to stop. This is especially true if you have never meditated or it has been a long time.

I like to start by stretching all of my muscles and breathing deeply. You will begin to feel your mind calm down and your thoughts become clearer. The tension of my mind usually ends up in my muscles, so stretching relaxes my muscles first and my mind follows. Once I get into this state, I sit calmly with the best posture I can be in. I spend the next five to ten minutes breathing and allowing a deeper state of relaxation to become more present. At this point, I pray. I'm very much in the moment to allow myself to see and hear my purpose. It helps me feel more centered, and I can approach my day more calmly. The whole process takes less than forty-five minutes. It takes practice, but with time you will start to see the benefits. Give it a chance and if you need to laugh at yourself, don't be afraid.

The most successful people hit adversity and they stumble, but there is a way forward. There is a way back. You have the power to take down the brick wall of the negative perceptions that block your way forward. You hold the power to transform each dismantled brick in that wall from a roadblock into a road, the road through adversity.

Chapter 8

CIRCULAR ADDICTION

Why do some lives move in circles?

You see a friend from high school or work, who years later, seems to be the same exact train wreck they were a decade before. They make the same errors, have the same Debbie Downer attitude and limiting beliefs, and it seems as if they're just repeating the same year over and over. If this is you, it's time for a wake-up call. The definition of insanity is doing the same thing over and over again, expecting different results. You can't expect your life to suddenly turn for the better without you personally making an effort to break the cycle.

Have you ever made the same mistakes over and over? Getting in and out of situations and doing it all over again is a circular process. Some people do this for decades, while others just get sick and tired of the cycle.

It may be overeating, being lethargic, drinking too much, or not working out. You may have a set goal to start something but haven't yet. Why do people live in these cycles when they want to break free? I believe it's because so often we don't know who we truly are and have lost sight of what our ultimate goals are. When this happens, outside influences are determining the choices we make, or we cover up pain or boredom with our addictions.

If it feels good, we do it. If someone else is doing something that sounds fun, we follow. The goals fade from being personal to trying to make other people happy. It may be that we haven't even set a goal for ourselves. One thing I know for sure is that I don't want my child to be addicted to anything, and that means I have to do my best to remain sober and educate my family on how to live a healthy life. I am having to make the deliberate decision to break my own cycle of addiction.

What causes us to get trapped in a circular cycle? Not growing and learning through our negative experiences and getting trapped in a daily routine of bad habits. Sometimes marriage, kids, your job, and what seems like the same day happening over and over can lead us into depression. Making the wrong choice of friends and losing focus on what is important is another.

What does it take to break this cycle? For us to make a change, it usually takes a traumatic event to force us to make a choice. A death in the family or a sickness. Divorce. A car wreck. Anything that can snap you out of the trance of the repetitiveness of life. But wouldn't it be great if we could break the cycle before something major happens in our life? When is enough, enough?

The day that changed my perspective and snapped me out of my circular addiction was when my wife took my son and left me. I had spent years getting drunk and stopping and then repeating it. I had gotten myself stuck in a routine of playing golf, drinking beer, and hanging out with my buddies. I wasn't focused on a goal or how I was representing myself to other people. I had checked out and just wanted to have fun.

The worst thing about it was I didn't even notice until I got so drunk, I didn't remember coming home. I woke up in the floor of the shower at 6 a.m., hung over, and with no memory of what had happened the day before. Shannon was furious, and she took Palmer away from me. For one night, she left and that's all it took for me to wake up. How did I get here? I had been on a steady climb of improvement. I had set goals and was meeting them one at a time. I was doing so many positive things that I got complacent. It was time to get focused and bounce back in a positive way.

Life moves a lot like the stock market. Support and resistance. It has peaks and valleys, but it should always be making a slow climb and moving up with time. We make mistakes and sometimes become complacent. Support levels are our low points. Our support levels are where we want to bounce back. Resistance is our high point. Resistance is the level we want to break through. As we start to reach our high, we can get confident and then something knocks us off our upward trend. We are now on a downward trend, and we have a choice to bounce off our former learning experiences or sell ourselves short.

We have discussed how life is a continuous learning experience, but some people never learn. You are mortal, and you made a mistake. If your last mistake was solved by going and getting drunk, shopping, or overeating, and you do it again, you learned nothing and are selling yourself short. What do you get when you drink to solve a problem? A hangover and a problem. If you face the problem in a completely different way like exercising, asking for help, or admitting your humanity, you will bounce off your support level and hopefully to a new high. You are smarter, wiser, and becoming a more mature human being. It's not that you are worthless. It's that it's a good time to bounce back and go to a new high as a better person. When we get stretched and are meeting our goals or achieving our version of success, it's easy to become overconfident or complacent. We peak. We don't believe that anything can possibly knock us off this run we are having. Bad days happen, and we can learn or we start the circular addiction over again.

Unforeseen events happen, and we can't control all of these variables. You must reorganize. Maybe your process was flawed before and now you know what to fix. You learn and keep bouncing back, each time higher and higher. Just like the stock market!

How do we bounce back? It can be easy to get stuck in your relationships and the routine of daily life. It can stop you from moving forward. Even with the constant ever-changing environment when you have a successful career or a growing family, you can forget to take care of yourself.

That is when depression or the unforeseen can creep in. No one is immune, and it can be a big stumbling block for a lot of people. Many of us don't realize that we have reached the point where depression is a part of our lives until we have hit the bottom as hard as we can. Maybe the friends you hang out with are the wrong group of people. They can bring you down or suck you into the drama of their life instead of building you up. You must put yourself into a more positive circle of friends who can motivate you to continue to strive to be better and to grow instead of just living that circular process. Be ready for those negative people to not want to let go of you. It's easy to say change your friends, but actually doing it may be one of the most challenging things you have to do.

That will give you the strength to pour into others too.

When we are making the same mistakes over and over again, most of us don't even realize that we're doing it. It takes that epiphany moment or someone you trust saying, "Hey, do you know you aren't supposed to be doing this over and over again?" to wake us up. It may seem so simple, but often we are our own worst enemies, hitting the wall and refusing to acknowledge that we hit it, and hard.

When I was in therapy, the psychiatrist would ask me questions about stepping out of my comfort zone. I would always respond, "I'm not ready to do that; I'm not ready to do this." One day, he asked me, "What would it take for you to make a change?" I said, "I don't know; I never thought about it. I don't know." I began to ask myself, "What am I doing here and where do I want to be? How do I get myself out of this? Am I happy with my current place in life?"

This moment of reflection and desire to change will accelerate you to the path of growth instead of stagnation or being trapped on the same level and just repeating it over and over and over again. I started with setting small attainable goals. Then intermediate goals. Then long-term goals. Starting with baby steps of small changes is leading to an entirely new way of life for me.

When you are ready to start moving out of that infinite loop, build a plan. What do I want out of the next six months or twelve months and then begin working toward that goal. Remove the distractions. Learning how to deal with and remove distractions gives you the momentum to reach the goals you are setting. The noise in my life was really hard to block out, but that didn't mean I could use the noise as an excuse to fall back into bad patterns. I didn't respond to it in the same way. I was reaching healthier choices and learning to face the situations as they happened.

Replacing the negative energy was a big step. I became able to take my energy and put it into a positive life-improving project. Working out, gardening, yoga, art, meditation, going to church, or donating your time to help someone else are all positive steps. Pick one personal activity a day and focus on yourself. Don't try to do ten things because you will most likely fail and have to start over again. It isn't a perfect system, and of course it's easier to feel sorry for yourself or to be negative. It is important to pick something *you* love and not something your family or friends love. You have to have the personal drive to get out of bed every day and go do it. You have to recognize your patterns and find a solution that works for you. Recognizing my tendencies to be negative, then finding the solution, was a long-term project. Remember that habits take at least two weeks to form, so stay at it.

Your brain will heal with time. Your thoughts can be re-programmed from reaching for your addiction to making a healthy decision. When, after many years, I chose to stop drinking, I found it humorous to be around people who were drunk. My perspective had changed, and I saw how people change after just a few drinks. I looked at myself differently and was proud of the way I was approaching life. The circular addiction had been exposed, and I knew how to deal with it more appropriately.

The biggest thing to breaking my circular addiction was me saying "no more." It was me putting me first and saying I want more for myself. No one else can make this decision for you. Are you ready to break the cycle?

THINGS TO TAKE ACTION ON:

- List your addictions:

  1.

  2.

  3.

- What addiction on this list could you live without?

  _____

- What action can you take today to insert a positive habit into your life?

Chapter 9

BALANCE

What does balance mean to you? It can be defined is many ways, but most people look at the word balance by describing the way they are "balancing" their home life and their professional life.

To me, balance is looking at your life and understanding that you have the right amount of perspective on the value of your time and where you spend it. What kind of time are you devoting to your family, to your spirituality, to your work, to your relaxation time, and to your hobbies?

It is so easy to find ourselves all consumed with work, work, work. I found that I began neglecting all the other parts that could have made my work-life easier. I was giving up family time because of a fear that if I spent any time away from my work, or away from thinking about baseball, or working out, that it would affect me negatively. Another way of saying it is that I felt outside influences would be a distraction.

My days melted into every other day, and instead of feeling like I had time to enjoy things, there was really no balance in my daily or weekly life. It was work all the time, stress all the time, and focus on success all the time. Instead of being able to step away and play golf or spend time with friends or family or

John Patterson

take time out on Sunday, I was buried in work. It is a slippery slope when you find yourself dedicating all of your time to just one avenue in your life. It will lead to a complete burnout.

People say to be successful, you have to sacrifice. But how can you sacrifice your time with your family for your career? How do you find a balance? For me, I never had a spring break or went to a happy hour until after I retired from baseball. When I hung out with the players after the game, all we talked about was baseball. We were all consumed with baseball and nothing else. I was raised to think about not getting married too soon or not having kids too soon because it would be a distraction. It was built into my head that I can't do this or I can't do that. I surrounded myself mentally with what I couldn't do. All that did was make me focus on baseball and not have any moments of peace or time to de-stress. It made me consume my life with only one thing, and I felt overwhelmed if someone tried to get me to do anything else.

If there was one thing that I did do, it was go to baseball chapel in the dugout on Sunday for fifteen minutes. This was the only chance I gave myself to find some type of balance, but that wasn't enough.

If you sat down right now with a sheet of paper and wrote out your day, what would it look like? This is a great exercise to show you where you are spending and losing your time. It gives you a better perspective on what your daily routine is and what it should be. Are you distracted at work and not getting enough done so that you have to bring your work home with you? Are you letting other people control your time because of the issues they want you to focus on? Are you scrolling through social media or watching TV to pass time?

How do you create that time and make it count?

It is all about margin time. Scheduling your day removes the possibility that you didn't make time for something that is important to you. There is wisdom in prioritizing your day and focusing on getting your priorities done by noon. Then you can spend the remainder of the day putting out fires for other people. This can help prevent you from getting to the end of the day and still not accomplishing your priorities for the day.

It's definitely a discipline. Of course, taking responsibility for your schedule is a learned skill. But over time, you will become more disciplined, and it will give you the space in your day to accomplish the things that are truly important to you. If you find that you feel like you don't have time for what is important to you, then evaluate what you want to do and plan your day.

I'm going to get up, eat breakfast, meditate, and go to the gym. When I finish with all of that, I go home to work in my office. Whatever it is you want to do, schedule it. By scheduling out my day, I was able to use the margin time I had left to pursue my hobbies, like golf. Hobbies are not a waste of time. You are taking some time for yourself to do something you enjoy. It may be that you just need to take a walk, something that allows you to de-stress and detox. When you are running a hectic schedule, making sure you have it mapped out can be the one thing that helps you keep your stress down.

Throughout this book, I have taken you through my journey to find a healthier me. Having a routine keeps me healthy. For me, the randomness of things is not good. To me, randomness causes anxiety. But having a plan, being prepared, and having the discipline to follow the plan allows me to relax and get rid of my anxiety. That doesn't mean that creating a schedule can't cause you problems. With anything, you have to be flexible. As I build a more rigid and tighter schedule, I can find myself obsessing. I can give myself deep frustrations because (as with anything) there are positives and negatives with scheduling.

All life requires some measure of discipline. As you begin to make priority time in your life for different things, you are exercising a new discipline in your life. It means you are taking the things that are important to you and making sure they are not optional. For example, going to the gym is a discipline, and eating healthy is a discipline. In everything, you know what you need in your life, and you know what you don't, whether it's a tighter schedule that you follow or a looser schedule. Or maybe your peace and comfort is found in the random. Whatever gives you peace, plug in the art of discipline to actually maintain it.

Discipline is an art. It is you taking responsibility for how you are going to live your life. My wife is a master at discipline. Every day, her alarm goes off, she goes to Pilates, comes home, eats a healthy breakfast, showers, and spends her day in her office. Her day is scheduled out, and it is a pattern that she follows consistently because she knows that keeps her mentally and physically in the right space. It becomes easy, as long as you don't obsess over it.

Balance is an excellent goal, but it can be bad and become an obsession if you don't give yourself grace. In anything, you have to give yourself room for growth and change. When I go to the gym and focus on just lifting, not lifting anything necessarily heavy, but just lifting, I get in the movement of working on my body and allowing my endorphins to kick in. I leave the gym feeling good and ready for my day. I feel accomplished and healthy at the same time. That is a good thing because feeling healthy is something that works for me and helps me feel like I am working on the part of my life I can control: me. When the extremism kicks in and I want to lift more and more and more, the weight keeps going up and up and up and up and up, and eventually it gets to the point where I can't stop messing with it. If I don't find a natural stopping point, I will take it too far, pull a muscle, or injure myself. Then the discipline and fun I had before is now something I not only have to recover from, but it is a chore. It changes the way I see something that keeps me healthy.

After my baseball career ended, I still had a competitive spirit. I could not throw a baseball, but I could swing the golf club. What started out as a hobby and something to get me out of the house became work. I thought maybe I could repeat my success I had in baseball on the golf course. I started going to the driving range and hitting balls for three hours every day to work on my swing and physical conditioning. I would watch videos of drills to practice and take lessons, pushing myself more and more. Golf was supposed to be my hobby, but now I was turning it into an obsession. I knew I couldn't play on the PGA tour, but what about amateur tournaments? The next thing I knew, it wasn't fun anymore. I was approaching it as a job. That's not why golf was there. It was to help me relax and enjoy myself, not obsess over. I guess it's just my personality to push myself to the maximum and see how far I can go. My wife had to step in and say that I had taken it too far before I would stop. I still play, but I only play to have fun and relax. That's what a hobby is supposed to be.

In anything, we always have to remember that we are our own worst enemy.

Finding peace in balance

Knowing that we are our own worst enemy, we have to depend on having outside influences who can point out when we become the most detrimental factor for ourselves. My outside influence is my wife. I need that outside influence to say, "Hey, you need to calm down. You need to take it easy, not stress so much or push so hard." She can see when I have set my expectations too high and I am starting to expect too much of myself. That outside influence can give you a clear line of sight when everything becomes cloudy with your expectation. That different perspective will actually help you catch those moments when you go overboard quicker than you used to be able to. My wife is a voice of reason when I don't notice it, and everyone needs that person in their life. I need my wife when I'm starting to feel differently or think differently, or even talk a little differently. She will always point out if I am starting to get more aggressive. It is as simple as, "Hey, you're getting a little aggressive." Of course, my first response is, "No I'm not! I'm not like that." That answer alone now snaps me back to reality.

The search for continuous balance and peace is ongoing. It isn't something you attain and everything is fine. My wife and I are in a constant discussion about me trying to find peace and balance. When you are in that space and searching for someone to help you with that journey, make sure they are someone you love and trust. You need an honest person to be able to give you the feedback as you go through the process of trying to become better and more balanced.

Creating belief in yourself and your ability to create goals and a schedule that helps you achieve the life and business balance you are looking for takes time. You have to create realistic goals and build your day to include the elements that will help you succeed.

Success can be achieved in a lot of different ways, and everyone is different. There is a myth behind accomplishing your goals. It doesn't create immediate happiness. Ask someone who is successful and has accomplished all their goals, "Are you happy?" Most will tell you that they have created more and newer goals because they are truly never able to find the happy in just being. "I have all this money and fame, and I'm not happy" or "I am confused about where I am in life." This is a direct reflection of not being in balance. You may have everything you want, but you have no home life, you have no true friends, and you have no other things that bring you happiness. Why? Because your life is way out of balance. Now you have to take the time to really look inside yourself and find out what your priorities are.

There are so many things that can throw off a schedule, and they can build a sense of chaos and anxiety into your once solid and peaceful life. The thing that throws me off is change. Change and spontaneity make me crazy. To me, change has always meant lack of control. I like being able to know what's going to happen and when. I guess you could call me a creature of habit. I've never been great at accepting a change in my schedule. During my baseball career, when my family would come to town, it would change my routine. I was happy to see them, but I really did not enjoy having to focus on something else for a few days. That's a horrible thing to say, but that's how unbalanced I was. I had lost perspective on what mattered the most: family.

We all have bad habits that get our lives out of balance. In my life now, I still don't like change, but I deal with it differently. I compartmentalize my priorities. By doing this, I can take out the bad habits and insert the good habits. My focus is on God, family, finances, fitness, and hobbies. It has taken many years to get my priorities in that order. It takes trial and error, but stick with it. Twenty years ago, it would have been baseball, fitness, baseball, and baseball. That was not balance. That was an obsession.

If you are ready to break the habit of bad patterns, you have to first follow them. My bad patterns always started with drinking alcohol and not having a relationship with God. Figure out what your bad habits and patterns are. Then you can combat them. Good habits that create peace and balance have structure. They help you take the structure and build healthy habits. Habits are things that help us stay on track, but give yourself grace.

Boundaries also play an important role in your balance. If you have something that doesn't have a purpose in your life and you are not setting a boundary, you are getting distracted from yours goals and getting more out of balance. A good example I used earlier was playing golf and drinking alcohol. If I used the golf course as an escape and a distraction, it really wasn't serving a purpose for my long-term goals. If I go to the golf course with the idea that I am going to relax or network with a business partner, then I am using golf in a healthy and balanced way. It is the exact same environment, but with a different perspective and focus on my priorities and goals.

Another big part of setting boundaries is learning when to say no. First figure out why you need to say no. Does the item you are saying no to add any value to your life? Is it helping you reach a goal? Is it adding quality time with your family? If the answer to one of these or all of these is no, then you most likely don't need it in your life. A lot of people get dragged into activities because they feel pressured by a group. It is easy to get caught up in a moment and feel like it is the right decision at that time, but then you need to take a moment to yourself and evaluate if it is contributing to your life.

There is nothing worse than saying yes to something if you can't make it to the end and complete the task. You don't want to be known as the person who doesn't complete a task or follow through. People will respect you more for saying no than not following through. You also don't want to spread yourself so thin that you are never fully present in the activity you are doing because you are always having to think about the next thing on your list. Your family and employer will easily take notice if you are distracted and can't be in the moment. This is a good reality check that you need to start prioritizing and cutting out the things that aren't adding value.

What are your priorities in life?

Are they really in the order you wrote down or is that how you would like them to be?

Do you see change as a positive or a negative?

Chapter 10

BUILDING A TEAM

In order to build a team, and in order to be successful through adversity, everything you build has to start with a strong foundation. That team is part of your foundation, and you can reach out to them when you need it most. The relationships you build will give you the strength to reach out when you are weak, but also allow you to reciprocate when someone on your team needs you. Your team needs to cover all aspects of your life. For me, that includes my family, faith, fitness, finances, and close friends.

Many times, we think we can just do things on our own. I was a strong-minded athlete and had a negative character trait of believing I could just do it all on my own. The thoughts that race through your mind are cliché.

I'll just do this on my own.

I don't need anybody.

I can make this happen.

I'm good enough to make this happen.

There are a lot of things that you can do on your own in this life, but it is being immature and overconfident to think you understand everything. Think about anything we do and do well. How did we learn the skill? Was it a coach who pushed you? A coworker who cheered you on? I know that nothing happens alone. Even having a coworker who you don't like, but who is really good at their job, is teaching you something. If we are honest with ourselves, we know that we are not doing it on our own. There's always somebody there who is motivating you or helping your run, whether you realize it or not. The quicker you can realize some of those things, the more you start to realize, "Hey, I can be so much better if I would just open up and allow people to help me if I ask for help."

What Is a Team?

Team can be defined in so many ways. I consider my wife a part of my life team, and I have many people close to me who I trust to tell me the truth. Most people would call their friends or even their acquaintances part of their team. The truest definition of team is people in your life you would share your most intimate secrets with. How many people do you know who you would share the most important things going on in your life? Most people have two or three. It isn't a large number because if we are honest with ourselves, it isn't easy to be fully open and vulnerable with people, especially if they aren't close.

Choosing the Right People for Your Life

Having a partner and someone who holds you accountable is extremely important. For me, that's my wife and my mother. Between the two of them, they can pick up on the little things I may not have shared with them. My mom has always had an extreme intuition of knowing if something is going on with me. It is a sixth sense that very few people can understand. She will get a feeling and immediately call me and ask, "What's going on?" That alone will get me to spill on what is currently dragging me from my peace. Her immediate response is, "What were you thinking? What were you talking about? What were your thoughts?" She runs through those questions, and it is an immediate boost to put me back into my normal state. It gives me the jump start that helps get me back into my routine if I misstepped.

The first step to finding the right teammates is to understand your needs and the needs of those who are important to you. What gets you out of balance? I know drinking too much would shift me off track. If I had a drink every day for a week, I wouldn't feel as good as usual. It isn't that I am hungover; it is the accumulation of drinking every day. It makes everything feel off. It will change some of your thought processes. This is where that accountability to someone else comes in handy. When my wife points out, "Do you realize that you've had a drink every night this week?" it is a wake-up call for me. I don't realize when it is that frequent. It's not binging, it's one or two a night, but being self-aware and realizing what you are doing on a more conscious level takes a lot of time and discipline. It is why having the right people around you, who can be honest with you will help you reach your goals and help you stay in a healthier space of balance. We all are looking for an advantage in life. There is no magic pill to take. The closest thing is to have good team of people around us. Just remember that you can't be the only one receiving in a team. You also need to look out for the people who are looking out for you.

You can't do it on your own.

I am grateful to say that I have more than most. I know I have people that are not only family, but close friends that I feel comfortable with. I could call my brother, my sister, my parents, my wife, and then I have two or three other friends that I could call and feel comfortable with sharing if I was struggling. The gift of being open and honest is priceless.

This realization made me truly believe that everyone must have a team of people they can share life with. I know I would have died if I hadn't had my parents to call that night in 2003. I know that I would not be as happy as I am now or able to get through situations that I struggle with daily, weekly, and monthly if I didn't have my wife. It is easy for people who don't know your full story, or just know the CliffsNotes version to say, "It's going to be okay" or "You're overreacting and it's not a big deal." You need to be able to connect with people.

Something that I could never have predicted would be the way my son has impacted my life. Seeing him and seeing his eyes when he sees me or when he wants to sit next to me makes my life complete. I get that feeling of complete acceptance, being wanted, and being loved. Being openly appreciated for no reason gives us that sense of being complete. I know most people are looking for that feeling. They want to feel complete. I know I did. Before God, there was always something missing.

Having the right people around you allows you to be more content and grateful with where you are in life.

When I look back at what it looked like to have friends who were athletes, I only had two teammates who I would truly call friends during the entire time I played. Ben was another high school player from Texas. We played our first three years together. He was an eccentric guy from Austin, but we had a lot in common. We were roommates in Double A in El Paso and went everywhere together. He always made me laugh and could tell a good story. We leaned on each other. I could tell him what I thought and how I was feeling, and he did the same with me. Ben kept me calm and helped with my anxiety. In 2001, I was rehabbing from Tommy John surgery in Triple A, and Ben was sent down to Double A. Ben had begun to show signs of being bipolar. He went to Wichita to play a game and he disappeared. They couldn't find him. He booked a flight to Canton, Ohio, and went to the Pro Football Hall of Fame for a reason no one could figure out. He broke into the football stadium and slept on the field that night. He somehow made his way to Cincinnati and found a cop car. He opened up the back door of the car and climbed into the backseat. The police asked him what he was doing, and Ben replied that he wanted to go to jail. They continued to ask him questions until they found out who he was. They were able to put him in touch with his family and flew him back to Austin.

After a few months, I vouched for Ben to the team, and they allowed him to come back to Tucson and live with me. We went out one night in Phoenix, about ninety miles away. Ben disappeared at some point while we were out at a club. We started looking for him that night and kept calling his phone. He wouldn't answer. The next day, I covered for him with the team and said he was working on some stuff and would be back soon, but I didn't know if he was dead or alive. I spun myself out of control worrying if he was okay. Two days later, the doorbell rang. I opened the door to find Ben barefoot with blisters on his feet. He had walked the ninety miles from Phoenix to Tucson without any shoes. He wouldn't tell me anything and then went into the guest bedroom, laid on the floor, and stared at the ceiling. The next day, we told everyone what was going on. He flew back to Austin, and I never saw him again. It was painful for me to lose Ben. I had leaned on him, and he was the only teammate that I ever had that deep of a friendship with.

The pain of losing Ben isolated me, and I didn't want to get that close to another teammate again. I was grieving the painful loss of a friend and didn't know how to handle it in a healthy manner. I had a sense of camaraderie with other teammates, but no friendships ever penetrated below the surface of the game. I wasn't able to reach that level of friendship again until after my career ended.

As teammates, we suffered together through the crucible of the season, and no one else knew what that experience was like. You would create relationships, but they were only surface deep. It didn't matter if you weren't friends with all of them. You were a team. If someone fights your teammate, then you fight too. I had teammates I didn't like who I would fight for, especially when it was game time because as a team, you depend on each other.

You don't realize how much you want and crave a truly intimate relationship with other people. You take it for granted that you are already part of a team. And while it may not seem intimate, you spent all day watching film together. You would spend pregame getting taped. We spent time in the whirlpool and in the training room getting iced. We spent 24/7 together, but in reality how much did we really know about one other?

You run into the problem that, in reality, you all have different personalities and different views on life. You know you would definitely fight for them and play hard for them. But in the end, there wasn't a connection. This can be the same in any work or corporate situation. You spend time together because part of your job is to be with those people every single day. Most of the time, you spend more time with them than you do with your family and friends. In any work relationship, there is a certain amount of strength you show. For many people, your coworkers won't know you inside and out like your family and your closest friends that you've had for years.

The downside to this false intimacy is that there is no freedom to be able to let go of all that we are hiding, and to unload and decompress. You are truly unable to answer that question, "How are you?" or to honestly answer, "This is how I'm feeling, this is what I want, and this is where I want to be. Can you help me figure out how the heck I can pull this off?" Knowing you have a team of people you can confide in and you can tell the full honest truth to keeps you from pulling away. The opposite of that is what put me in the worst situation I've ever been in. I pulled away from that aspect, pulled away from my loved ones, and pulled away from my closest friends who knew me the best. And then ultimately, I pulled away from my teammates. I built a cocoon around myself with very thick layers. That is not the way to success. It was what led me to nearly lose it all. I had to come to grips with where I was and finally reach out. Being able to be open and free comes through having close relationships. Only then can you become able to talk about who you are and how you feel.

Do You Have the Right Team?

It can be hard to build a support system, and not all of us have a family we can fall back on. Many times, you have to step out of your comfort zone and create new connections with people, some of whom you may have never considered becoming friends with.

The biggest thing you have to remember is that ultimately some people are going to let you down. Just remember that all of us are human and deserve a chance (or maybe second chance). But you have to try, you just have to be able to reach out. I wanted to be able to have people I could talk to about those personal feelings, not just about work, like how I hadn't had a drink in a month, or where I was mentally. I wanted to be able to escape the work conversations. I wanted to have those deeper levels of communication like the way I enjoyed my relationships with my parents, my brother, and my sister.

I truly realized the benefit of that separation once I got married. When I married my wife, I started spending less time with the guys and more time with her. It became much easier for me to decompress because there was a true separation from work when I was home with my family. It gave me the chance to just be me.

If you don't have this separation of the two, it can create conflict even in your own head. How do you get certain thoughts out of your head? You need someone to bounce crazy thoughts off of in order to hear, "Hey, you're overreacting" or "Hey, it's going to be okay." Sometimes that's really all you need.

On the baseball team, and even in the corporate world, the goal is to win. There isn't always a feeling of genuine care about how you are. The lack of trust is inherent, and sometimes it's the coworker who wants your job. They want your position. Can you trust what they're saying to you? It is a tough call. You won't always make the right judgment call on whether it is a safe bet to trust them. You just have to follow your gut and make the best decision.

During those first stages in any relationship, you will always wonder if you are sharing too much or not enough. For the longest time, I had trouble sharing my past. Now, I can share that I had a problem with drinking and drugs when I was younger. The response I see is people opening up and sharing their own stories. Maybe it was a situation they were in that wasn't good or they went through a divorce. The openness of my conversation has given people the space to be real and human. People will like you for being a real and honest person. That is a simple step, so just be real. Be who you are and understand people are still going to hurt you or let you down, but that's on them, not you. Remember that you can only control how you react to them.

You may say you have twenty friends. But actually you probably only have three true friends and seventeen people you have a great time being around. The point is to not retreat from those other seventeen, but to know who those true friends are. Recognize those people who you can fully trust and lean on. It is important that you know those are the ones you can call during your tough days and who are going to give you the feedback you need to hear. They are going to be the ones who help pick you back up and get you back on track. When you are riding out this crazy life of ups and downs, they are the ones you need to invest in.

To invest in yourself, you need to build your entourage. They are the sphere of people who can protect you, guide you, and support you to help you invest in yourself. They always say hindsight is twenty/twenty, so let's play a game. If I could go back and do it all over again, this is how I would build my team. I would begin by building my support structure, which was my mom and dad. For every home stand that was more than a few games long, I would have had my mom or dad or both with me and when available, my brother and sister. My dad always helped me with my game plan, mechanics, and thought processes. My mom was always the one who gave me the feeling of love, and I could talk to her about everything. They were my conscience when I couldn't hold myself accountable. They would have helped me destress and would have given me some separation between baseball and life.

I would have hired a financial advisor earlier on in my career to set a budget and hold me accountable to my long-term financial goals. I would have hired my personal trainer full-time and brought him with me to Arizona. He would have given me meal plans, exercise routines, accountability, and balance. I would have continued to build my faith and to continuously learn about the Bible. It would have allowed me to focus on the gifts God had blessed me with and the opportunities He was giving me. I would have hired a sports psychiatrist who I would have spent a considerable amount of time talking to each month. He would have stopped me from overanalyzing my mistakes and kept me from trying to figure things out on my own.

Yes, it would have been expensive, but it would have kept me on a more balanced and healthier track. This team would have helped me to achieve the short- and long-term goals I set for myself. This could have taken a tremendous amount of stress and pressure off of me. They would have allowed me to continue my education of life and baseball, develop in a healthier way, and not make as many self-inflicted wounds and mistakes.

There were quite a few people who would comment about how the amount of money I signed for was too much too soon. In many ways it was, but not the ways you think. It was about the isolation and the mentality that I must know what I am doing. Mistakes were made because I didn't make the right decisions about building my team around me. I let out-side influences affect me negatively by telling me what they would do if they were me. I didn't have the confidence yet to stand up and say this is what I need because this is how I got to this point.

Don't be afraid to stand up for what you believe; surround yourself with great people, and go for your dreams.

Who are the people around you who push you toward your dreams?

Who are the people holding you back?

Are you listening to outside influences that are negatively affecting your judgment?

Who are the one or two people you can add to your team to help push you to the next level?

Chapter 11

ATTITUDE IS EVERYTHING

There is an underlying theme in this book, so I am going to address it straight on. Attitude is everything. Attitude is the way you approach your day, project, team, and life. If I get up in the morning and say today is going to suck, it is going to. If you are positive and have a self-belief that you are going to crush the day, you will. Small things won't get in your way. You are approaching your project and leading your team in a positive way by your positive attitude. The perception others will have of you is this is the person I want to be around or lead me. They will see you as someone who is ready to work, to have a good day, and to get things done.

I played with a guy one time whose nickname was "Electron" because he was negatively charged. It would be a beautiful day, and he would find something negative about it. No one wants to be around a person who brings your mood down. It is hard to be successful with a negative attitude.

If you let your environment affect you, you will in return become your environment. I don't believe people are born negative. Life experiences have affected that person in a way they don't know how to deal with, so they put a wall around themselves. I think back to when I was in high school. I see

127

a young kid who was like a sponge to everything around me. I was always the young guy because my talent put me in an older group. I don't want this to sound like an excuse, but that environment greatly affected me.

I was a sophomore hanging out with a bunch of seniors who didn't have the best standards. Being a West Orange-Stark Mustang was about being aggressive. It is a blue-collar type of attitude toward everything. The seniors weren't always the best role models because they had negative habits, didn't like school, and they were bullies. I absorbed their mentality and thought it must be okay if they are doing it. I didn't have that personality, but it started to isolate me because they didn't want to hang out with me already because I was young, so I did what I thought I had to do to fit in. I also went home every night to it. My dad could be aggressive, and we all walked on eggshells around him. There was nowhere to run from it.

The attention from the scouts and the media started to build, and it took a giant toll on my friendships and my relationships with my coaches and teachers. It is a rare occurrence for this amount of attention to be directed at one person in a small town. My friends were jealous and didn't want to be around me. My coaches resented the amount of calls, mail, and scrutiny they were under. I was forced to make a choice if I was going to let their negativity affect me or if I was going to keep it from hurting me. This is when the wall started to go up, and I began to not trust people. I was building a shell like a turtle. I would stick my head out every once in a while, but I really wanted to stay in that shell and be protected. My attitude went into survival mode to protect me from getting hurt. It was me against the world.

I went into pro ball thinking everyone was going to work together to accomplish the same goals, and I was finally going to know what it was like to be on a true team. But I quickly learned this was not the case. It was every player and coach for himself. This affected my attitude even more, and the wall continued to get higher. I thought the team's management was going to protect me, but instead they threw me out to the wolves without any protection. I went deeper into survival mode.

When I was in El Paso in 1999, my coaches cornered my dad when he came into town. They were asking what was wrong with me. My dad responded and said, "You all are with him every day. You should know what is going on." They told my dad I was moody, reclusive, and didn't want to be a part of the team. They had noticed I began to withdraw from everything. I didn't have the relationships I wanted and the leadership I needed from the team. My coaches and teammates took my reclusiveness as being cocky and arrogant, but it was more about me not having self-worth and not being comfortable in my environment. It was a culmination of all the negativity and hurt I had experienced from the last five years. My attitude was tough for anyone to be around, and I was okay with it isolating me.

The accumulation of injuries took my attitude to another level because the injuries were holding me back from meeting my full potential. My self-worth only came from throwing a baseball and trying to be perfect. Being hurt messed with my psyche, made me depressed, and I beat myself up. When all of it came to the point that I was going to need surgery, it was the accumulation of years of depression and poor attitude that lead to my addictions. It was a snowball rolling down a hill that became an avalanche. At this point, it would have been okay to grieve and be sad about the outcome. My attitude should have bounced back and been about how much better I was going to feel and be after surgery. But that is not what happened. My attitude never bounced back. The grief never went away. The deeper I got into my addictions, the more I questioned if it was worth giving effort into changing my attitude because I was ashamed of my response. My friends didn't want to be around me because I was on drugs, and my attitude was piss poor to say it in the least. I didn't want to be at the field, I didn't want to work out, and I didn't want to try. My attitude and actions pushed my team and coaches away and isolated me from the world.

Baseball is not much different from the corporate world. There is always someone standing in line chomping at the opportunity to take your place. They are waiting on that misstep, so they can come in and save the day. Your team doesn't have time to stop and wait for you. They have to continue on to hit their quarterly numbers or secure the next big deal. In baseball, being on the Disabled List (DL) was like a plague. You are playing baseball with some of the most superstitious people in the world. When you are hurt, they don't want to be around you because they feel like your arm injury would somehow rub off on them. And let's be honest, when you are on the DL, your attitude is usually not the best. The combination of the two can be very isolating and make it even harder to get healthy and back in the rotation. The team has to move on. They don't have time to wait for you to get back up. They have to take the next guy gearing for your spot and run with him. I have always said it is an individual team sport. You are in one day and out the next.

It wasn't until I hit rock-bottom and lost almost everything that I realized if I changed my attitude and perspective, I could get it all back. This is when I became motivated to pitch my best to be traded, and I started rebuilding my relationships with my family. I started to believe "I can do this again" and change my attitude. When I got to Montreal, I had the right coaches with Frank Robinson and Randy St. Claire and the right general manager with Omar Minaya. I had good friends on the team who were positive and helped me believe in myself again. I had the freedom to rebuild my mechanics and confidence because I had a positive attitude. I had the will to succeed again and felt like I put my dream back within my reach. It was a place for me to let go of my past and rebuild my idea of success. All of this happened because my attitude had changed to one of being open and accepting. I finally wanted to be part of a team again.

But as I have talked about several times in this book, life is a cycle. I had everything together and was coming off one of the best years of my career and in an instant everything changed. My life went on a different path than I saw coming. I had another injury to my elbow, but I was pitching through the pain. My fourth start in 2006 season against the Florida Marlins, I struck out thirteen batters for the second time in my career. That night on SportsCenter, Scott Van Pelt said "This guy can pitch, by the way." I remember thinking that I had put myself back on the map in baseball. I was right where I wanted to be.

My next start was against the Atlanta Braves and John Smoltz. It was another strong outing for me. After that game, my arm was in a tremendous amount of pain and I went on the Disabled List. A few weeks later, the manager for the Atlanta Braves, Bobby Cox, ran across the field to ask me about my nerve injury. He knew who I was and respected me enough to care about me being healthy. I had fought the battles and put myself back in the position that I had always dreamed of, namely being respected as a baseball player. I had another surgery that off season and came back as the 2007 Opening Day Starter. Then in an instant, all of this was taken away from me, as I needed my third and final surgery. This affected my attitude on life. I went down a deep dark path of trying to figure out life's great questions. Why me? What did I do to deserve this? Why did this guy succeed and I didn't?

It took me years to recover, to change my attitude, to stop asking "why did this happen to me?" and to start thinking about life after baseball.

Sometimes it is a personal choice of how am I going to approach my life. Some of it stems from being grateful. Yes, I lost the potential of millions of future dollars, a World Series Championship, a Cy Young Award, and many other top awards, but that world is gone. There was no alcohol in the world that was going to bring it back. When I finally got rid of my negative attitude and addictions, I could finally move forward and be grateful for the life I do have and will have. I have surrounded myself with positive people and positive experiences. There is nothing I enjoy more than going with my wife and son to volunteer at Halos special needs T-ball. This was something I had been avoiding because of my negative attitude on life, but now I look forward to spending that time with my family, giving back. I can now acknowledge the things I do have in my life instead of focusing on what I don't have.

I think back to my high school baseball coach and can remember to this day the overwhelming sense of resentment I had for him constantly chewing at me. It built a sense of mistrust and resentment toward him and didn't motivate me at all. He was supposed to be the person building me up, not tearing me down. You'd think coaches like that didn't exist anymore because of the archaic mind-set, but they do, in schools and leagues and fields across America.

There is enough research out there that coaching or teaching from a negative perspective is not the best way to do it. Being motivational and positive helps achieve better results in the long term because it's not about the one game in front of you. It's about the entire length of a lifetime and legacy. Leaders build people up and help them discover their gifts and utilize their strengths.

The reason I coach from a positive perspective is because of all the negative coaches I had growing up. I try to build up a pitcher's confidence because they are putting in the effort and have a positive attitude. If they are not giving me the effort, I point out the reasons they are not seeing success, like not practicing or doing the drills during the week. I don't make them feel worthless or like a failure because I have yet to see a positive response to these types of coaching techniques.

My wife and I are sponsors for Night of Superstars. It is an annual charity event in Dallas/Fort Worth that celebrates children who are affected by varying types of disabling conditions, yet reach far beyond their adversities by excelling in areas, such as academics, athletics, the arts, and community service. These children get a day to feel like celebrities by having a makeover, getting dressed up in a gown or tux, riding in a limo, walking the red carpet, signing autographs, and receiving an award on stage. These kids approach life with a positive attitude and believing anything is possible. They are inspiring because they don't let their disability or circumstance dictate their view of life. Every year, I am amazed when I am at the event by how positive each and every one of them are. We are all motivated and inspired by their example.

Anything is possible with a positive attitude and outlook on life. If you're feeling stuck, get up and get out and volunteer to help someone today. You'll be amazed how your attitude changes for the better!

Chapter 12

GRATITUDE

For most of my young adult life, I was not aware of all of the positives in my life. I dwelled on everything that was not perfect and saw the negatives as my destiny and reality. I didn't yet know that you are not your emotions. Your worst day isn't you, and your worst feeling isn't you, but just a feeling. I'm not sure why I put so much pressure on myself, but I did, without realizing it. This innate pressure to succeed was something that I lived with from a very young age.

If I colored outside the lines in kindergarten, I was angry and crunched the paper up into a ball and threw it away. Everything had to be perfect. Where did this desire for perfectionism come from? I have no idea, but I know it's been a driving force in my life.

I was living the dream of every young baseball player and could not be happy. If I pitched well, I focused on the mistakes that would have made it better. If I pitched poorly, I told myself I sucked. I was not grateful for anything—not my family, my wealth, my God-given talent, or my ability to get up and live the life I had always dreamed of. I wanted to be a pro baseball player, but in my mind I had dreamed it to be perfect.

When I was forced to retire, I couldn't move on because my accomplishments were not exactly the way I had envisioned them. In a way, I was pouting, but in reality my view of life and my career was wrong. I hadn't managed my expectations properly. This is what trips a lot of people up. Managing your expectations and understanding that curveballs are ironically a part of life is one of the most important things you can do for yourself. Manage expectations to prepare for the unexpected things that occur in life. You've got to be resilient and willing to pivot.

How do you move on after a tragedy or struggle? How do you modify your mind-set so you can be more aware of your critical self-talk? How can we all start today to make that shift from an improvement mindset to let's not be so hard on ourselves? Peace is the new goal. Forget about achievement and all of the mistakes of the past. What if you just measured your mind-set in terms of peace? Focusing on this one thing and asking myself these hard questions is a major key to transformation.

How do we get to a place of peace? How can we be grateful and allow our reality to be more in focus? Your mindset matters and you've got to make the decision to be grateful each and every day. We move on by changing our perspective and perception of ourselves or the situation we find ourselves in.

In my life now, I do my absolute best to not look at what I don't have or what I could have done better. I accept the reality that nothing will be perfect, and I only live one day at a time. I do the best I can and let it go. I focus on my wife and son, and where I'm going with my company. I'm focused on the correct things that actually matter, not lost chances of the past. Living one day at a time allows me to not become overwhelmed, which allows me to not become depressed. I say to myself, "It's just one day" over and over when things aren't going well. Another thing I have done is I have adjusted my perception. I realized I was doing so many things for other people to tell me "good job." As humans, we like to feel like we are a part of something, and sometimes we desire gratification from others more than anything. Have you ever stopped to consider why you were doing a certain action? Is it because you wanted a "pat on the back" or because you were doing it for yourself?

My life changed drastically when I started shaking out the actions that were for the approval of other people. This is a huge problem in society today. Oftentimes people are not even authentic about why they're doing something. They do it because someone else is doing it or for the approval of others.

I grew up before social media had taken control of our culture. I'm very grateful for that. People today are comparing themselves to how other people present their lives on social media and telling themselves they are not enough. You are enough, but you aren't focusing on what you do have and what you are grateful for.

After my second year in pro ball, I was starting to grasp the amount of money I had. I started to feel like I could do anything I wanted to do because I could afford it. Before I was drafted, I didn't understand the value of a dollar. But around this time, I started to feel what it was like to have money. My personality had started to change, and my persona started to form into the baseball player. Everyone around me was saying if I were you, I would do this. If I had all that money, I would buy this. I started to let everyone's opinions affect me. They started to shape John the baseball player. One of my other teammates that year had a red Dodge Viper. That was the sports car to have at that time. They were widely popular. After the season, I decided I was going to buy one for myself. It wasn't that I needed it or even truly loved the car. It made me feel good to be able to say I could buy it because I could afford it and do it just because I could. There are situations we all get into because we have the mentality that we can do whatever we want. I never once stopped to think about why I was buying the car or if it was for the right reasons. The car was rough and loud. Being 6'6", I could barely fit in the car and had to turn my head sideways just to drive. I couldn't take it with me for the season because I couldn't fit anything in it. During the off-season, I couldn't drive it after my leg days workouts because my legs would shake so badly, I couldn't push the clutch in to switch gears. Driving a race car down I-10 in Houston traffic was not practical because it didn't have anti-lock brakes. The car was so fast it was actually a little scary to drive. It may have had a few thousand miles on it after three years. It mostly sat in my parent's garage collecting dust before I finally sold it. It made me feel good for maybe a few months after I drove it off the lot, but all it really did was create a larger emptiness I was trying to fill.

Find a quiet place and write down ten things you are grateful for. Then, write down ten material items, trips, or things you think you just can't live without. Put them in an envelope, and in thirty days open it up to analyze it. I would be willing to bet the things you are grateful for mean more than the material or dream items. You might even ask yourself, "What was I thinking? Why did I want that?" When I have done this in my life, I've always been amazed at how dumb the material things are on the list thirty days later. They don't mean anything, and I usually felt I would like to have those things because of spontaneity or I was trying to feel better about myself. It doesn't work like that.

Stuff will never fill up your emptiness, and if you aren't grateful for who you are at the most basic of levels, you will stay empty forever. This test gives you a better perspective of what life really is about. If you end up wanting the material items more than the items you are grateful for, maybe you should check yourself a little harder. You can't have peace living like that. If there are a few things on my list like a new watch or a vacation, I use those items as motivation to work toward as a gift for myself or family. It's a reward, not something I need to be happy.

As an athlete, the ability to make fifty thousand people get up out of their seats to clap and cheer is an adrenaline rush that is hard to replace. For the longest time, I looked for something to replace that excitement, but it's not possible. Not exactly. I realized I should be grateful for all the times I was able to feel that excitement. My chasing the feeling of trying to repeat that emotion was causing me to not let it go and be grateful I had the opportunity to experience what it was like. I got to stand on a Major League mound and strike out Barry Bonds, the greatest hitter of all time. The first five times I faced Barry, he was in the prime of his homerun-hitting years, and I walked him four times. I was more than happy to pitch around him and just let him walk to first base.

Over the next six at bats, I got more aggressive with him. I don't really remember the first time I struck him out. I could not tell you anything about the at bat other than I think it was a fastball on the outside corner. The primal emotion of what that is like is hard to explain. It feels like electricity flowing through your body. Your senses are heightened to the point your hair is standing up and you can feel the blood pumping through your veins. The next game I faced him, I remember it like it was yesterday. It was in Washington, DC, at RFK Stadium late in the season, and he was chasing Hank Aaron's homerun record. The stadium was packed, and my game plan was to pitch him hard away and breaking balls down in the dirt.

In his first at bat, I got ahead of him and decided to throw a cutter at his back knee. That had been a very successful pitch for me all year. If the batter hit the ball, it was a foul ball or a very weak ground ball usually. If they didn't swing, it would be so far inside that it would make the hitter move his feet and make him become more uncomfortable in the box. It would set up my next pitch. I felt like it was a good time in the count to make him move his feet so that I could throw a fastball away on the next pitch. With one runner on, I came set and threw the pitch exactly where I wanted it and he promptly hit it out of the ballpark. I just shook my head.

He had gotten me. I was one of the 449 pitchers he had hit a homerun off of in his career. But, in his next two at bats, I struck him out. His second at bat was a fastball away, and the third at bat was a curveball in the dirt. I was jumping around and screaming like I was being stung by a bee. He just glared at me. It was awesome, and I get excited writing about it today. What an experience it was to face the best ever, and I will argue with anyone who says otherwise. It can't be replaced, and I shouldn't try. If my goal was to face the best hitters in the world and strike them out, I accomplished that. We can't replace some of the best moments in our lives, but we will always have the memories. Let's be grateful for them.

For the longest time, my baseball career was not what I had viewed as successful. Most baseball players would give anything to play one day in the Major Leagues. I got to play for years and along the way, played for and with Hall of Famers. These are dream situations if you can be grateful for the opportunities. Being held back by injuries clouded my perception and didn't allow me to see it clearly.

Frank Robinson is one of the greatest baseball players to ever play the game, and I got to play for him. Frank was the only player to be named MVP for both the National and American Leagues. He was a fourteen-time All-Star. Frank was the first African American manager in big league history and was elected into the Baseball Hall of Fame the first year he was eligible in 1982.

Frank was a baseball legend! The more I learned about him, the more he inspired me. Frank was able to get the best out of me because I didn't want to let him down. He could look at me and I knew what he was thinking. He was a funny guy and had a great sense of humor, but was a very serious person. I enjoyed being able to sit and talk to Frank, about anything. He was the first manager I had in pro ball who I felt cared about me.

In 2006, my arm was in a lot of pain, and Frank knew it. He had to take me out of a game against the San Diego Padres. He came over, sat down on the bench, and put his arm around me. He wanted me to tell him what was going on. He had pain in his face because he knew I was hurting. He truly cared about me, and my career in a way that I had never felt before. I never had a coach who truly cared about me and it meant everything to me.

He had always inspired me because of the obstacles he had to overcome during his career from racism to not having a place to stay and eat. Then, he went on the field and performed at the highest level. It always made me try and get into the frame of mind that Frank had, to be so focused and take my aggression out on the opposing team. I would tell the media I was trying to play the game the way Frank would. He would read my quotes then come find me, punch me in the stomach, and tell me thank you for the kind words. All of the pain and hurt I went through was nothing compared to all the obstacles Frank went through. I am grateful I got to experience playing for a legend and being someone Frank Robinson cared about.

My family is what I'm most grateful for. I can't imagine the pain and confusion I put them through. For them to stand by me and always be available when I needed them is something I will always have gratitude for. My dad, and this is hard to say, has always been right in the advice he has given me. My mom is the most compassionate and caring person I know. She loves me unconditionally. My brother and sister have supported me every step of the way and given me the honest truth when I needed to hear it. I have so much to be grateful for. It just took a long time for me to recognize it.

I understand everyone doesn't have family that supports them. If this is you, please recognize the one or two people in your life who have influenced you in a positive way or have been there when you needed them the most. Good relationships are the hardest to find and also the easiest to take for granted. Being able to take a step back and acknowledge these people in our lives or send them a thank-you note can bring us back to the right state of mind.

To not be held back by addiction is the greatest gift I have ever given myself. There were times in my twenties and early thirties that I believed I would always be addicted to something. It had become part of my daily routine, and I never went anywhere without smoking a joint or at a minimum having some whiskey. Anxiety and depression, along with no sense of purpose, had done a number on my psyche. Facing the world wasn't what I wanted to do and admitting I had a problem wasn't going to happen. I remember having good days and saying, "I need a drink." Then having a bad day and saying, "I need a drink." What is the point of this way of thinking? What is the point of alcohol? If you need a drink to celebrate an accomplishment or a drink to relax when you have a bad day, you are not in control of your life. I know I wasn't.

When I was able to see the addiction was dictating my day and making my decisions for me, I became free. I've always enjoyed challenges, and this has been one of my most long-term challenges, to become free of addiction and thinking I need a substance to get through the day. To break free, I began focusing on the blessings I have and the consequences of losing all of those blessings if I didn't stop. It's not that drinking doesn't cross my mind; it's that I resist the urge because I have challenged myself to find another way to "have fun" or deal with a problem. It's not necessary because I'm grateful for my life. If you are struggling with addiction, challenge yourself to focus on the blessings in your life.

In the winter of 2004, I played in Santo Domingo, Dominican Republic, in the Winter League. I had torn my groin in Montreal and missed some innings during the regular season that I needed to make up. I had a good year but wasn't as consistent as I needed to be. Pitching in the Dominican was an opportunity to build my confidence and grow more consistent from start to start. I was excited to go and always wanted to play in that league. It was filled with up-and-coming big league players.

The biggest eye opener for me was the surroundings, to see what it is like to play in a country surrounded by poverty. You don't truly understand poverty until you have been in a Third World country. I grew up hearing stories about how ecstatic these kids were just to show up at the field every day because it is a huge upgrade from the lifestyle they grew up in. Many of the kids don't go to school, and the way they survive is by walking the street trying to find something to eat. The youth players would train at the fields, and they would be rewarded with fruit at the end of the day. This is how a lot of these players got their start. They don't have cleats, gloves, or much less a uniform.

It is a different view of baseball than what I grew up with. Here in the States, it is recreational. In the Dominican, it is survival and their only chance to make it off the island. I played on better fields in high school than I did in the minor leagues. But when you compare it to the Dominican kids, it wasn't in the same ballpark (literally). They were playing on fields covered with rocks with gloves made out of milk cartons. I was so confused in the minors, playing on what I thought were horrible fields and second guessing why I didn't go to LSU.

When I questioned my dad about it after my career was over, he said he didn't tell me what the minor leagues were like because he didn't want to cloud my decision. He wanted it to be my decision because it was my future. But at the end of the day, my dad, protecting me, set me up for a false perception of what the minor leagues were all about. I was making $850 a month in the minor leagues. An interesting side note is my dad made the same amount when he played in the 1970s. But to the players from the Dominican, it was the most money they had ever made and they were grateful for every single penny.

When I arrived in the Dominican, they handed me a list of rules of what I could and couldn't do for my safety. I had a driver who would pick me up and took me to and from the field or anywhere else I wanted to go. I wasn't allowed to walk around, especially outside my hotel. Food was sketchy, and I had to be aware of what I was eating. I would go to this one pizza shop every day. These kids would stand there and wait for me. They were never in school and always around. I would go in and order pizza because that was the little Spanish I knew. I would eat a few slices while they would watch me outside the window. When I was done, I would go outside and give them the other half of my pizza. They would follow me around everywhere I went. They knew I played baseball and I would feed them. I couldn't wrap my mind around being in their shoes.

All the Dominican players had guns. When they would come in the clubhouse, they would take their guns, remove the magazines, place the guns in the padlock boxes, and put the magazines in their pocket. The box would be locked up until after the game. They would unlock the box, pull their guns out, load them, and then walk out. It was like the Wild West the moment you walked outside the gate. It always made me wonder why I didn't have a gun. All of the Dominican players would tell me I didn't need one because I was American. It was a different world seeing people walking around with shotguns over their shoulders.

The positive of all this chaos was their passion for playing the game. It was like good old-fashioned sandlot baseball. I didn't feel pressure. It was fun and I was healthy. Because of that, I pitched really well. I was the most dominant I had been in many years.

The fans fed my confidence. They responded to me, and it was a feeling I had been longing for. They were waiting for me after games and followed me around the city. It filled a void that I had lost from being injured. It was the confidence I needed to help bring everything back together and get me back on track. I was grateful for the opportunity to love baseball again. It reminded me of why I loved to play the game. There was joy again in something that had been drowned out by the business side of the game in the States. There was no media in my face tearing me apart. It ignited my passion, and I was ready to tackle the world again.

There is something to be learned when you watch the difference between how a Dominican player and a player from the States play the game. The Dominican players play with passion, joy, and love. They want to be on that field, and they are grateful for every second of it. It gave me a different view of myself and my career. When I left the Dominican, I truly believed I was going to have the best year of my career in 2005. With the different perception of myself, I did have the best year of my career. For the first time in a very long time, I believed in myself. I owe a lot of my success of 2005 to my time in the Dominican.

It's a rare occasion when our lives are truly awful. It happens, but most the time we are just overreacting to normal everyday life events. We come home telling our spouses how we had the worst day ever. I hit every red light. My client is stupid. My boss is an idiot. Yep, I've done it. Now it is time to switch those thoughts. What if you approached it with a positive and grateful mind-set?

You have a spouse to come home to and vent about your day. You have a car to drive you back and forth to wherever you need to go. You have clients who are contributing to your business. You have a job that is paying your bills. How different would your life be if you went from "having" to do something to "getting" to do something? The next time you feel yourself getting frustrated with having to do something, take a moment and focus on what you are grateful for.

Being grateful is about being open to opportunities. It is having the right attitudes and perspective to put you in a position for the next great thing in your life, like facing Barry Bonds, striking out Hall of Famers, playing for Frank Robinson, and being in the right frame of mind in the Dominican. All of these things set me up physically and mentally to have the best year of my career. It put me in the right place and time to meet my wife, which placed me where I am now. It is about the future opportunities that you don't even know are there yet. If you let a setback hold you back, you are missing out on the incredible future that those setbacks are leading you to.

END OF CHAPTER EXERCISE

• Write down five things you are grateful for.

_____

_____

_____

_____

_____

What are five positive qualities you possess?

_____

_____

_____

_____

_____

How can you become more open to new opportunities?

_____

_____

_____

_____

_____

LET IT GO

This is a letter from me to you. Now that you've read my story and struggles, I want to encourage you to take a big massive step toward Peace today. It's time to put your past behind you. It's time to forgive yourself or whatever it is that's holding you back. Holding onto the past is not making you better and it's not allowing you to become your best version. We all have failures and traumatic experiences that we need to overcome, and we need to commit to starting our new lives right now.

I started changing my perspective six years after my career ended. I realized that my life was more than my expectations of myself as a baseball player. That part of my life was over, and there was no going back, no matter how much I wanted to go back and change it. I also realized that I needed new motivation to pull myself out of depression. That motivation is my wife and son. I focus on them and what their needs are and what kind of example I want to be for my son. Slowly, but surely, I noticed how I was getting better and my life had meaning again. I didn't need to drink alcohol anymore. I didn't need approval from the outside world anymore. I didn't need to feel alone anymore. I was letting go of my past and focusing on my future. You can too, if you find your motivating factor. Quit focusing on your former self. Let it go.

As my perspective changed and I had a new motivation, I felt like my perception of who I am and what my purpose is became more evident. I forgave myself and could see that everything of value in my life is because of my successes and failures. God granted me an amazing life, and I could be grateful for all of His blessings only after I forgave myself. I had been successful and because of my failures, I was in the right place at the right time to meet my wife. It's easy to look backward and say if I hadn't made that one mistake, I would be in a much better place. That's not true because you absolutely do not know that. God saved you; you just didn't recognize it at the time. Your perception of yourself can only improve if you forgive yourself for your mistakes. Stop letting the past dictate to you who you are. It's just life. Let it go.

On Palmer's first birthday, my wife had all of our family and friends write letters to him that he would open on his eighteenth birthday. In my letter, I promised him that I would be the best I could be. This became my long-term goal. My expectation is that I will be the best role model I can be for him and that my marriage to Shannon will show him what love is. I can give him the tools to be the best he can be because I have had both success and failure. My wish for him is that he will not be too hard on himself, like I was, and that he can have the right perspective, perception, and perseverance.

I now define myself by my day-to-day actions. I try my absolute best to stay in the present. I still have a long way to go, but I realize that I will never achieve all of my goals. I now understand the difference between a "want" and a "need." I have a relationship with God that I have never had before, and it brings a joy to my heart like I have never felt. I am alive for the first time in my life at forty-one years old. There is happiness in my life that I didn't believe I deserved for more than twenty years. Now, every morning I wake up in a beautiful house, next to an amazing wife, with a wonderful son, and I wonder how I became this blessed.

I want to be a positive force for people struggling with addiction, depression, anxiety, and failures. There are people in our lives who are struggling, and we don't see it. I pray that God can use me to help people realize that there is hope and that they do deserve happiness. I am an example of what can happen if you can "Let it go."

By forgiving myself and letting go of my past, I am able to dream again. I am allowing myself to experience new opportunities in fields I would never have put myself in before. I will make some mistakes and experience some new setbacks, but with my new foundation, those hurdles won't throw me off track. I am excited to live and experience life. It's like God gave me a second chance, and I am running with it.

What one thing are you ready to let go of?

What new passion would you like to pursue?

If you didn't have that one thing holding you back, what would you want to accomplish?

ABOUT THE AUTHOR

John Patterson is a speaker, author, and father who lives in Prosper, Texas, with his family. He speaks to organizations and individuals on managing adversity, change, teamwork, and overcoming unexpected challenges. In his senior year of high school, he was a First Team All American and a Gatorade Player of the Year. John was selected as the fifth overall pick in the 1996 Major League Baseball Draft by the Montreal Expos and was the first high school player drafted that year. Playing at the highest level, and having immense potential but being held back by injuries that sidelined his baseball career, created the perfect change management coach anyone can relate to. His message is "It won't be easy, but it's worth it to push through adversity and find the real you." John's story will inspire and challenge you to find the right perspective and the positives in your life.

NOTES

NOTES

NOTES

NOTES

NOTES